How To Think About Law School

A Handbook for Undergraduates and Their Parents

Michael R. Dillon

ROWMAN & LITTLEFIELD EDUCATION
A division of
ROWMAN & LITTLEFIELD PUBLISHERS, INC.
Lanham • New York • Toronto • Plymouth, UK

Published by Rowman & Littlefield Education
A division of Rowman & Littlefield Publishers, Inc.
A wholly owned subsidary of The Rowman & Littlefield Publishing Group, Inc.
4501 Forbes Boulevard, Suite 200, Lanham, Maryland 20706
www.rowman.com

10 Thornbury Road, Plymouth PL6 7PP, United Kingdom

British Library Cataloguing in Publication Information Available

Library of Congress Cataloging-in-Publication Data

Dillon, Michael.
How to think about law school : a handbook for undergraduates and their parents / Michael Dillon.
p. cm.
Includes bibliographical references.
ISBN 978-1-4758-0245-0 (cloth) — ISBN 978-1-4758-0247-4 (electronic)
. Law schools—United States—Admission. 2. Law schools--United States. 3. Undergraduates—United States—Handbooks, manuals, etc. I. Title.
KF285.D55 2013
340.071'173—dc23
2012040744

™ The paper used in this publication meets the minimum requirements of American National Standard for Information Sciences Permanence of Paper for Printed Library Materials, ANSI/NISO Z39.48-1992.

Printed in the United States of America

To Mary Ellen (1943–2006)
in memory of
your love, patience, and courage

Contents

Preface   ix

1 Pre-Law Undergraduates—Majors, Majors Everywhere   1
  1.1. Follow Your Passion I   1
  1.2. No One Right or Wrong Choice of Majors   3
  1.3. Dual Majors Are Not Necessarily Better   4
  1.4. Follow Your Passion II   5
  1.5. Save Your Successes   6
  1.6. It's OK to Decide "No"   7

2 Your Mission Freshman and Sophomore Year   9
  2.1. GPA Foundations   9
  2.2. A Myriad of Options   10
  2.3. It's Not on TV   13
  2.4. Ask, Interview, Shadow, and Visit   13
  2.5. Pre-Law Programs and Advisors   15
  2.6. Disciplinary Disclosures   16
  2.7. Question 1—How Much Will It Cost and How Do I Pay for It?   17
  2.8. Question 2—Why Such High Levels of Lawyer Dissatisfaction?   18

3 The Time Table Junior Year   21
  3.1. Counting Backward   21
  3.2. The Friday before Thanksgiving   24
  3.3. Test Prep, Test Prep, and More Test Prep   24
  3.4. Timing of the LSAT   25
  3.5. LSAC Accounts   26
  3.6. Letters of Recommendation   26
  3.7. Resumes   28
  3.8. Personal Statements   29

3.9. Waiting for a Year or Two   31

4 The LSAT   33
4.1. Prep Courses—Do I Need One?   34
4.2. Test Day—It's Not as Short as You Think   35
4.3. The Nature of the Questions   36
4.4. How Much Preparation is Enough?   39
4.5. But, Can't I Take It Again?   40
4.6. What to Know about the Scores   40
4.7. The Night after the Test   41

5 Choosing a Law School—"Know Thyself"   43
5.1. What Not to Do   44
5.2. Areas of Emphasis   44
5.3. Law School Rankings   45
5.4. Websites to Know   47
5.5. All the Same but Different   48
5.6. Careers Can Change   49

6 How Do I Pay for It?   51
6.1. Don't Count on Scholarships   51
6.2. Tuition, Books, Living Expenses Equals?   52
6.3. Like Buying Your First House   54
6.4. Interest Rates on Loans   54
6.5. Your Debt Limits How and Where You Can Practice   56

7 The Law School Application Process   57
7.1. LSAC Account   58
7.2. LSAT Score   58
7.3. Undergraduate Transcript(s)   59
7.4. Personal Statement   60
7.5. Letters of Recommendation   60
7.6. Resumes   62
7.7. Early Decision   63
7.8. Addendum Dos and Don'ts   64
7.9. Disclosures Advertent and Inadvertent   65
7.10. How Many Applications   66
7.11. First, Second, and Third Tiers   69
7.12. Forget Rankings Most of the Time   70
7.13. The "Wait List"   71

8 Acceptance—The Holy Grail   75
8.1. I Can Breathe Now   75
8.2. Visiting Schools—Stay the Day   76
8.3. What Is My Long-Term Goal?   76
8.4. Where Can I Flourish?   77
8.5. The Summer before Law School   77

8.6. Proposals for a Legal Reading Plan 78
8.7. Proposals for a Nonlegal Reading Plan 78

9 The First Year—There Are No Second Chances 81
9.1. Transition and Success 81
9.2. Curriculum and Briefing 82
9.3. The Reading Load 83
9.4. Socratic Method 84
9.5. Study Groups or Not 85
9.6. "Thinking Like a Lawyer" 86
9.7. Outlines 87
9.8. Examinations 88
9.9. Law Review 89
9.10. Second-Year Interviews 90
9.11. Clerkships 91
9.12. The Summer after First Year 91

10 Second Year 93
10.1. The Curriculum 93
10.2. Law Review 94
10.3. Interviewing for Summer Associates 95
10.4. Clinical Programs 98
10.5. Moot Court and Mock Trial 99
10.6. Elective Courses—Winnowing Down Options 101
10.7. Competitive, Confident, and Cordial 102
10.8. Summer after Second Year—Summer Partners 102

11 The Third Year 105
11.1. Waste of Time? The Unnecessary Year? 105
11.2. Electives—Has Your Passion Changed? 106
11.3. Still Building Resumes 106
11.4. Networking and Faculty Support 107
11.5. Employment within a 150-Mile Radius 108
11.6. Remember: Your Debt May Limit Your Job Prospects 108
11.7. Summer after Third Year—You Are Not Bar Exam Ready 109
11.8. You Are Also Not Practice Ready 110

12 Lessons to Carry With You 113
12.1. Learning Every Day 113
12.2. Continue to Pursue Your Passion 114
12.3. Thinking Problems Through and Tracking the Details 115
12.4. Respect, Civility, and People 115
12.5. A Profession, Not Merely a Job 116
12.6. Doing Good While Doing Well 117
12.7. Stress, Success, Failure, and Family 117

Appendix A—Four-Year Checklist for Those Interested in Law School   119
    Freshman Year   119
    Sophomore Year   120
    Junior Year (In Many Ways This Is the Key Year)   121
    Summer after Junior Year   123
    Senior Year (Plan on September, October, and November Being
        Hectic)   124

Appendix B—Guidance on Letters of Recommendation   127

Appendix C—Successful Law School Application Strategy   129

Appendix D—Additional Readings   135

Afterword   139

About the Author   141

Preface

I think, and hope, this *Handbook* presents something of practical value both for the thousands of undergraduate students each year who are thinking about law school and a career in the law and for their parents. This *Handbook* can also serve as a resource for collegiate career counselors and pre-law advisors as well as for high school seniors thinking about careers in law and their guidance counselors, most of whom never attended law school. And it should be a useful guide to the many adults who change careers and consider law school later in life, as I did.

Two prefatory questions arise: first, "why another book about law school?" and, second, "why should the reader trust the author of this *Handbook?*"

In answer to the first question, there are plenty of useful books about law school in your college library, pre-law advisor's office, and local bookstores. These books fall into three categories: those focusing on the law school experience, especially the first year; those focusing on the yearlong law school application process; and those focusing on preparation for the LSAT examination.

This *Handbook* does not attempt to replace any of these quite valuable resources but rather provides undergraduates and their parents with a wider, broader, and longer perspective derived from my extensive undergraduate teaching and counseling background, attending law school later in life, and experience as a pre-law advisor as well as experience practicing law at a major national law firm for twenty-two years.

My goal in what follows is to create a reference book taking a student from the first week of freshman year, when he/she learns where the pre-law advisor's office is, through resume building, the LSAT, the law school admissions process, letters of recommendation and personal statements as an undergraduate, to the critical importance of the first year in law school, law review, the law school curriculum, clinical programs, summer clerkships, and interviewing for a first, full-time legal position.

The *Handbook* is designed to be accessible for students, providing useful, concrete, and practical information including lists of dos and don'ts, a four-year checklist, information about key web-based resources, and a step-by-step explanation of the law school application process, as well as a formula for successfully selecting "competitive," "safe," and "reach" law schools that increases your chances of admission. And, after addressing the pressures and opportunities presented by each of the three years of law school, the *Handbook* concludes with seven lessons to carry from law school into the beginning of your practice of law.

The second prefatory question, "why should the reader trust the author of this *Handbook*?" strikes me as a fair and pertinent question. I have substantial experience. I come from a family of lawyers (five consecutive generations, counting both Ireland and the United States) and was expected to become a lawyer. Back in the 1960s, however, I rebelled against the expectations that I would become a lawyer and instead went off to earn a Ph.D. and become a college professor in Philadelphia. I taught undergraduates in political science from 1968 to 1985, hundreds of whom went on to attend law school. During those years, I wrote hundreds upon hundreds of letters of recommendation to law schools. To this day, I remain friends with many of those former students, now successful lawyers, who are currently in public service, elective office, government, or private practice. Many of those former students are now heads of firms, senior partners, hiring partners, and in-house counsel both to major corporations and public entities. During those eighteen years as a college professor, my first publications appeared in legal journals like the *Baylor Law Review* and the *American Bar Association Journal*.

At age forty, I made the belated decision to attend law school. From 1982 to 1985, I attended the Temple University Beasley School of Law. Despite having a family and continuing my full-time teaching position, I made law review, became an associate editor of the *Temple Law Review,* participated in the school's Federal Clerkship Clinical where I clerked for Judge Arlin Adams at the Third Circuit Court of Appeals, spent a summer at the U.S. Attorney's Office for the Eastern District of Pennsylvania, graduated *magna cum laude*, and received both the Corpus Juris Secundum Award and the Raynes, McCarty, Binder Prize for legal research and writing at graduation.

Following law school, I joined the litigation section of one of the largest law firms in the world, Morgan, Lewis & Bockius, LLP, practicing environmental litigation, primarily Superfund cases. Throughout it all, I had a great time following my passion. I met wonderful clients and worked on cutting-edge cases. For a period of twenty-two years, I practiced in the federal courts of Pennsylvania, Vermont, Rhode Island, New York, New Jersey, Delaware, Ohio, Illinois, Wisconsin, Virginia, Florida, Texas, Arkansas, Tennessee, Missouri, Minnesota, Arizona, and California.

In 2007 I left the firm to return to teaching undergraduates. Since then, I have served as chairperson and professor of the political science department and as the coordinator of the university's pre-law program. I continue to advise students on the nature of legal practice, the demands of law school, the difficulty of the LSAT exam, and the overall law school application process. And I regularly attend meetings of the Northeastern Pre-Law Advisor's Association (NAPLA) and Southern Pre-Law Advisor's Association (SAPLA) to discover what other pre-law advisors around the country are recommending.

During my career, I wrote letters of recommendation for and provided advice to undergraduates who gained admission to all of the following law schools and many more: Harvard, Duke, Cornell, Texas, Virginia, Georgetown, Temple, Notre Dame, Pennsylvania, American, Dickinson/Penn State, William and Mary, Maryland, Rutgers, Wake Forest, Seton Hall, Villanova, George Washington, Roger Williams, Maine, Vermont, Albany, Fordham, Western New England, Boston College, Drexel, Pittsburgh, Widener, Pace, Baltimore, Loyola Chicago, Marquette, Catholic, Toledo, Akron, Syracuse, SUNY Buffalo, Miami, and St. John's.

In the substantive chapters which follow, hopefully, I convey to undergraduates my love of the law and my respect for the legal profession. But I am not a cheerleader. This *Handbook* openly discusses (1) the extraordinarily high cost of law school and the way law school debt can limit where or how you practice, (2) the two faces of the law discussed by retired Supreme Court Justice Sandra Day O'Connor as a ruthless bottom line business and as a profession where *pro bono* service must be rendered, (3) the shortage of opening legal positions for law school graduates following the 2008 recession, and (4) the continuing high levels of stress and dissatisfaction in the legal profession along with the growing problem of incivility and the difficulty lawyers experience finding a balance between their personal and professional lives.

The advice which follows is based solely upon my years of experience and my desire to offer advice that is comprehensive, practical, and as honest as I can make it for anyone thinking about law school. All errors of omission or commission are mine alone.

Chapter One

Pre-Law Undergraduates — Majors, Majors Everywhere

1.1. FOLLOW YOUR PASSION I

My basic message is that if you are truly committed to attending law school, you should "follow your passion." A legal career continues to be a very attractive option for many students about to begin their college or university studies. At the same time, in 2013 the law appears to have two faces—one noble and another not so noble. Beginning college undergraduates and their parents have all been exposed to lawyer jokes, which emphasize the law's not-so-noble face:

Q. How do you tell when a lawyer is lying?
His lips are moving.
Q. What is the difference between a lawyer and a vulture?
A lawyer gets frequent flyer miles.

Many of these jokes are not said in jest but are clearly meant as serious social commentary and criticism. Yet most lawyers view themselves as performing important and beneficial social functions—representing society's poorer members, establishing predictable rules for business and society, and resolving unavoidable human disputes without violence. In American literature, there are fictional heroes, like Atticus Finch in *To Kill a Mockingbird*, who portray the noble side of the legal profession. More importantly, there are actual historic heroes, like John Adams, defending the British soldier accused in the Boston massacre, and the archetypal Philadelphia lawyer, Andrew Hamilton, defending John Peter Zenger against the government's libel charges.

1

This dual face of the law is nothing new. Law as it developed in the United States was largely the inheritance of the common law of Great Britain. And it is worth noting that in England, William Shakespeare's and Charles Dickens's views of the law were just as low as the views of many citizens today. In *Richard II*, Shakespeare's antihero Jack Cade exhorts the rebels crossing into London, "first thing let's do, let's kill all the lawyers." In *Bleak House*, Dickens borrows the name of his fictional law firm from Thomas Hobbes's dark description of social life in sixteenth-century England—"Nasty, Cruel, Brutish & Short." Yet that same violent English heritage also gave us Magna Carta, the common-law rulings of Lord Coke, and the lectures of William Blackstone that provided the intellectual foundation and education for men like John Adams, Andrew Hamilton, and many of the American founders.

Despite this conflict between the dual faces of the law, the noble face of the law, if not victorious, at least, has never surrendered. During my twenty-two years of legal practice, my law firm provided support which allowed me to represent indigent prisoners in *pro bono* actions as well as to represent aged adults as *guardian ad litem*. I learned even paid legal work can have noble and beneficial outcomes. Two major corporations may be fighting over who holds the responsibility to pay for the cleanup of an industrial site with contamination caused by both corporations at different times. Serving as a mediator for the two can save time and litigation costs for both sides and allow the cleanup of the contaminated site to start as soon as possible. All of this benefits the everyday citizens who get a cleaner environment. Even with all the lawyer jokes, lawyers today—like doctors, accountants, bankers, and others—are treated as professionals in American society. Tens of thousands of college graduates each year apply to law school. In 2010 alone, 158,000 graduates took the Law School Admission Test (LSAT). Only about 63 percent of these students were offered admission to a law school. And the reality is that many of those admitted did not get accepted at their first, second, or even third choices. Furthermore, not all of those accepted ultimately enrolled in law school.

A natural question for college-bound students interested in law school and their parents is "if my son or daughter wants to go to law school, what should she/he major in?" As you will see, my answer once again will be "follow your passion." Colleges and universities offer majors that students were never exposed to in high school. This wide range of majors runs from psychology, to accounting, to special education, to finance, to nutrition, to sociology, to marketing, to environmental science, to philosophy, to economics, to comparative literature, and more. The larger the college or university, the greater the number of potential majors will be.

1.2. NO ONE RIGHT OR WRONG CHOICE OF MAJORS

While the question, "what should my son/daughter major in to have the best chance of getting into law school?" seems reasonable, there is no simple answer. If you want to become an accountant and earn your CPA, you major in accounting. If you want to become a reporter, you major in journalism or English. If you want to become a doctor, you major in biology. If you want to become a high school teacher, you major in secondary education. If you want to become part of an IT group, you major in computer science and technology. But there is no one right or wrong major for you to become a lawyer. I have advised majors in accounting, English, biology, education, and computer science successfully applying to law school.

A small number of colleges and universities actually offer pre-law majors, *but* most law school admissions officers recommend against such programs. Law schools want to be the one teaching their incoming first year (1L) students "how to think like a lawyer" using the law school's own methodologies. The fact is that undergraduate law courses, whether in "constitutional law," "criminal law," or "contract law," are not remotely equivalent to law school courses with the same titles, which use very different textbooks, assignments, pedagogy, and examinations. While you do not need a pre-law major at your chosen college or university, you do want to seek out a college or university with an active pre-law program providing resources, information, and guidance about legal careers and the law school admissions process to every student considering law school at all stages of their undergraduate career.

As an undergraduate, I was a political science major, but my father, also a lawyer, was a philosophy major and went on to become the chairperson of the American Bar Association's (ABA's) Real Property Section. Over the past five years, my university has sent students on to successfully attend law school from majors as diverse as political science, English, history, economics, accounting, American studies, communication, criminal justice, finance, environmental studies, sociology, philosophy, marketing, and psychology, among others.

Deans of law schools across the country as well as the creator and administrator of the Law School Admission Test (LSAT), the group known as the Law School Admission Council (LSAC), emphasize that there is no one right or wrong undergraduate major if you hope to attend law school. When it is time to submit your law school applications, generally in the fall of senior year, there are two key credentials upon which your application will succeed or fail—your undergraduate grade point average (GPA) and your LSAT score. At the start of your college career, there is not much you can do about your LSAT score, but there is a great deal you can do to establish your undergraduate GPA. By following your passion and majoring in a discipline you really love, you will work harder, read and study more, pay closer attention in class, and most likely earn better grades.

Undergraduates thinking about law school also need to understand that the Law School Admission Test (LSAT) is unlike almost any other graduate school or preprofessional test. The Medical College Admission Test (MCAT) tests what students learned in their courses in biology, chemistry, and biochemistry. The Graduate Management Admission Test (GMAT) focuses upon mathematical skills and the potential to succeed in graduate business courses. The Foreign Service Exam (FSE), administered by the U.S. Department of State, tests a candidate's knowledge of economics, politics, history, geography, and current events, among other things. The Post-Bachelor's Teaching Certificate in Pennsylvania requires testing in basic skills and subject competency. The Graduate Record Exam (GRE) for admission to graduate school offers specific area or discipline-oriented tests in chemistry, computer science, English literature, mathematics, and psychology. The GRE used to have field tests in economics, history, music, political science, and other disciplines, but has not done so since 2001. Since then, the Educational Testing Service (ETS) has offered a generic GRE for students interested in graduate school that tests vocabulary, analytical skills, analogies, sentence corrections, and mathematics. For all these tests, some majors are more useful than others to succeed on the graduate school admissions tests.

The LSAT, as we will discuss in the following, is different. It does not test any subject matter knowledge or any facts you picked up during your college career.

The LSAT is solely a test of logical or analytical ability, containing three types of multiple choice questions: reading comprehension questions, analytical reasoning questions (affectionately called "logic games"), and logical reasoning questions. Moreover, the LSAT is intentionally designed to mislead test takers by offering them "attractive distracter" wrong answers on nearly every question. Whatever major your passion leads you to choose, remember that if you are taking the LSAT and think anything from your major gives you an answer to one of the questions, that answer is probably wrong. So we end where we began. Follow your passion and major in what excites and attracts you, read a lot about your passion, and build your GPA from day one.

1.3. DUAL MAJORS ARE NOT NECESSARILY BETTER

Over the past decade, many students entering college, as well as their parents, became enamored of dual majors. Most colleges and universities permit dual majors, and some actively encourage them. From economics/political science, to English/communication, philosophy/literature, religion/sociology, history/foreign languages, computer science/philosophy, the potential combinations are almost endless. Dual majors "may" open more career opportunities than solo majors for undergraduates. But from my conversations with many law school admissions officers, I do not believe dual majors provide students considering law school with better resumes.

The reality at most colleges and universities is that to achieve a dual major, two consequences follow. First, almost all free electives are utilized to meet the requirements of the two different majors, thus students do not get the freedom in their junior and senior years to experience areas and disciplines where they may discover new and additional passions. My own undergraduate education would have been less significant had I not been able to take "Short Story Writing" and a course on James Joyce, even though I was a political science major.

Second, to guarantee that a student can meet all the requirements of two majors and still graduate in four years, most dual-major programs require each major department to waive one or two courses for the student who dual majors. Unfortunately, in most instances, both majors believe students need their foundational 100- and 200-level courses in order to be a major. Therefore, most dual major programs waive some of their upper division 300- and 400-level courses. Thus, when a dual major applies to law school his/her transcript contains double the number of freshman- and sophomore-level courses and much less evidence of the student applicant being willing to select more challenging junior- and senior-level courses.

From the perspective of building a powerful transcript, I would prefer that a student thinking about a dual major just select the one major she/he loves the most (follow your passion) and minor in the second academic department. Students can work with an academic advisor to build a "concentrated minor" which would ideally be composed primarily of upper division, 300- and 400-level courses. This approach builds a stronger-looking undergraduate transcript for a law school applicant.

1.4. FOLLOW YOUR PASSION II

Please do not forget your college or university career is a four-year opportunity to experience ideas, literature, fine art, technology, other cultures, books, languages, leadership roles, and service opportunities. This is a rare opportunity to develop both the scope and depth of your interests and your character. These four years can be—should be—transformative. More importantly, you cannot get these four years back. The next equivalent opportunity may not come until you retire approximately fifty years later.

If your college or university career is to be truly successful, you will develop multiple passions. You may come to love archeology, or the Mayans, or Abraham Lincoln, or classical jazz, or Latin America, or modern dance, or Annie Dillard, or the American Founding, or Stephen Hawking, or Mahler symphonies. The substance does not matter. Follow your passion whatever direction it takes you in, and remember the following comment from Henry David Thoreau, "Go confidently in the direction of your dreams. Live the life you have imagined."

By developing these multiple passions, you will ultimately be developing your future legal career. A legal career is a relationship business. To be a successful lawyer, you will need to relate to clients, partners, colleagues, opponents, judges, administrators, politicians, and many others. If the only thing you know and are passionate about is the law, you may technically become a fine lawyer. To form long-term close relationships with clients, partners, colleagues, and others, you will need to have shared interests and passions.

The client who shares your passion for jazz will connect to you on levels deeper than the law and "what have you done for me lately." The colleague who shares your passion for hunting may become the friend that sends you the case of your career. The senior partner who shares your passion for American history will find reasons to stop by your office and make sure you are included in the firm's biggest cases.

So it is important for you to develop and follow all of your passions. And, as we will discuss later, it will be important during your three years in law school not to let go of the passions you develop.

1.5. SAVE YOUR SUCCESSES

This advice is so important that it is repeated both in the next chapter and in the sections addressing law school applications. Applicants to law school will need to supply at least two and in some cases three letters of recommendation. For reasons to be explained later, your strongest letters of recommendation will come from faculty members, generally in your major, not from alumni of the law school you are applying to, not from donors, politicians, or even employers.

Law school letters of recommendation need to be detailed and specific. Faculty members teach hundreds of students each semester and expecting them to remember your specific performance on a project, a paper, or a final exam years after the course in question is simply not reasonable. Therefore, from your first day as an undergraduate, when you get back an exam with a note "one of the best in the class" written on it, or when you get back a term paper on Chief Justice John Roberts with an A+ on it, you need to safely file away and save your successes.

This way, when you need to approach faculty members at the start of senior year to ask if they would be willing to write letters of recommendation, you will be able to provide them with not just a resume and a transcript but with copies of finals, papers, or projects that the faculty member once praised highly but can no longer be expected to clearly remember. Your efforts at preserving your successes will assure that your letters of recommendation will have the detail and specificity to make them a valuable addition to your application to law school.

1.6. IT'S OK TO DECIDE "NO"

Many, perhaps most, students who enroll in a college or university planning on a legal career never actually go on to law school. Over the course of four years, many young men and women who initially considered a legal career decide they want to become teachers, engineers, journalists, social workers, accountants, entrepreneurs, policy makers, bankers, city planners, and the like. Other students discover that the dream of going to law school was perhaps more a dream of their parents for their son's or daughter's future than the student's own dream or passion. It is important to remember that at many colleges and universities, up to 50 percent of the students will change their majors. The four-year opportunity at the college or university to explore and grow intellectually, culturally, and personally will hopefully also lead to a productive and satisfying career. Therefore, both students entering college and university and their parents need to accept that it is "OK" to decide that you do not want to go to law school.

Even the young men and women who persist for four years with their dream of going to law school do not all go on to law school. Some of them will not build the GPA they need for admission. Another larger group will not obtain the LSAT score that will open the doors of law school to them. Beginning undergraduates need to understand that the size of law school first-year classes are much, much smaller than the size of freshmen classes in all colleges and universities. Most 1L law school classes contain only 150 to 300 students, not the 900 to 9,000 in most freshmen classes. In the fall of 2011, an estimated 19,000,000 students began college or university.

In recent years, an estimated 150,000 college and university graduates took the LSAT and applied to law schools for admission. Of those who applied for admission, only approximately 62 percent were offered admission. Of the group offered admission, not all matriculated in law school. Some accepted students did not get into the law school they desired and chose not to attend the lower-tiered school which accepted them. Others decided they could not handle the financial burden of law school debt, which for some students exceeds $180,000.

As detailed in the following, law school admission is neither easy nor certain. Since the economic downturn in 2008, law school graduates themselves are having a harder time obtaining full-time legal employment. Nonetheless, I do continue to believe the effort is worth it; as I say in the preface, I found practicing law very fulfilling and an opportunity for both service and continual intellectual growth.

Chapter Two

Your Mission Freshman and Sophomore Year

Your mission during your first two years at college or university is (1) to build your GPA, (2) to learn as much as you can about the range of legal careers and what occurs in law school, (3) to avoid the immature mistakes many college freshmen and sophomores make, and (4) by the end of sophomore year to begin seriously thinking through two critical issues—first, how will you pay for the high cost of a legal education, and, second, why there is so much dissatisfaction among successful lawyers at all levels of practice.

2.1. GPA FOUNDATIONS

During freshman and sophomore year, your first mission is to get the best grades you can. You will enroll in one-half of your undergraduate courses during these two years. Depending upon the college or university you choose, the vast majority of those courses will not be in your major. At many schools, those courses will turn out to be a smorgasbord of skills, humanities, sciences, and social sciences required in order to graduate. Freshman year is also a transitional year between high school and college, with students having much more personal freedom, elevated academic demands, roommate conflicts, social adjustments, leadership opportunities, and the like. Quite often good students, even Dean's List students by the time of graduation, struggle during their freshman year.

Ideally, you do not want this to be you. If you are considering law school as you enter college or university, you must understand that as far as your final GPA at graduation is concerned, your freshman year grades count just as much as your senior year grades. Actually, as you will see in detail in the next chapter, your freshmen year grades count more. If you want to begin law school the August after your graduation from college or university, you will want to have your applications submitted in late November or early December of senior year. Therefore, your official undergraduate transcript with the GPA which law schools consider is based on only three years of undergraduate courses.

A struggle academically during freshman year can dramatically impact that three-year GPA. Students who struggle freshman year often end up submitting an addendum to their law school applications which recalculates their GPA without their freshman year grades included. While this recalculation may have some positive influence on the law school's admissions decision, you need to understand that the American Bar Association (ABA) requires law schools each year to report the official GPAs and LSAT scores of their first year class.

Law schools do not get to send an addendum to the ABA explaining a low GPA freshman year; they must send your GPA "as is." The conclusion is quite simple: a low official GPA in your freshman or sophomore year can have serious negative consequences on your efforts to gain admission to law school.

2.2. A MYRIAD OF OPTIONS

Your second mission during freshman and sophomore year is to research what lawyers do and what legal careers exist. Most incoming freshmen, unless their mother or father is an attorney, have little knowledge of the immense range of legal practice. You cannot decide you want a legal career unless you have a fairly clear idea of what it is that lawyers do on a daily basis. There are a myriad of career options for students who graduate from law school. Some lawyers are in private practice; some are in government; some are not practicing law at all but are using their law school training "to think like a lawyer" in family businesses or as entrepreneurs.

Private practice includes solo practitioners and small, midsize, and big firm lawyers. It also includes in-house legal practice at businesses and corporations, large and small. A substantial majority of lawyers in the United States are in private practice.

Solo practitioners could be practicing in small towns, suburbs, or big cities. These solo practitioners can be in general practice where they provide business advice; prepare corporate filings; draft wills; handle estates, adoptions, and divorces; represent clients in real estate sales and purchases; and much more. Other solo practitioners only handle criminal matters; or work as solicitors for counties or townships; or specialize in only one or two areas of law (i.e., family law, real estate law, auto injury law, workers compensation law, and the like). As a solo practitioner, you control how you work and which clients you accept, but you run the risk of keeping your venture alive from rent to computers to paper and paperclips.

Small firms (ten to thirty lawyers) and midsize firms (fifty to ninety lawyers) generally engage in either criminal or civil practice but often do not do both. A small criminal defense firm may represent clients accused with a wide range of crimes from DUI, to possession of a controlled substance, to burglary, arson, and even murder. A midsize civil firm may be located near a county courthouse and handle a wide range of civil cases from contract disputes between businesses or landowners, to labor disputes between employers and employees, to personal injury suits against stores, buses, railroads, and the like.

Most small or midsize firms focusing upon plaintiff's work may be representing persons alleging injury in personal injury cases, while those focusing on defense work may be defending a business or company being accused of negligence or breach of contract. Some small and midsize firms are labeled "boutique" law firms, specializing in only one area of law (i.e., environmental law, immigration law, securities law, or intellectual property).

The size of a law firm heavily impacts the nature of your legal practice. Young attorneys fresh from law school will get more chances to handle matters independently and work with clients in small or midsize firms than they will in the large mega firms.

Large law firms vary dramatically in how large they are, measured in numbers of attorneys employed. At the low end, there are approximately 250 law firms employing more than 150 lawyers. At the high end, there are almost thirty firms employing more than one thousand lawyers, with the largest having over three thousand lawyers in seventy offices worldwide. At the high end, the firms are almost all "global" firms with multiple offices in multiple cities and countries.

In the United States, these firms are headquartered in major cities: New York, Washington, Chicago, Houston, Philadelphia, Los Angeles, Boston, Atlanta, Pittsburgh, Cleveland, and the like. Each firm is divided into multiple practice sections: transactional, litigation, labor, intellectual property, bankruptcy, regulatory, taxation, oil and gas, white-collar crime, real estate, environmental, trusts and estates, and many more. The major clients of these firms will include corporations—large, small and international, labor unions, railroads, newspapers, TV and radio stations, consulting firms, banks, hospitals, securities firms, cities, insurance companies, and the like. Many of these firms will take on both plaintiff and defense work. Attorneys fresh from law school generally will be hired in a specific practice section and will work for seven or more years under the firm's tutelage in order to be considered for partnership.

Private practice also includes in-house legal departments at institutions large and small, from oil companies, to retail establishments, banks, hospitals, nonprofits, pharmaceutical companies, mining companies, construction companies, computer firms, flooring companies, and so forth. These in-house legal departments can have from five to twenty attorneys who handle some matters in-house but who also hire and supervise outside lawyers from large and midsize firms specializing in areas of legal services the company needs.

In addition to private practice, there are a substantial number of government lawyers. Prosecutors at both the federal and state level are government lawyers. At the federal level, there are attorneys at the Department of Justice in multiple divisions including, but not limited to, Antitrust, Civil Rights, Drug Enforcement, and Environment and Natural Resources, as well as an Honors Program for high quality newly minted lawyers. Every Federal District Court generally has its own U.S. Attorney's Office which prosecutes federal criminal and civil cases in that district. At the state level, there are State Attorney General Offices at basically all state capitals as well as District Attorney Offices in basically every county and major city within each state. In addition, almost every federal and state bureaucratic agency hires its own in-house lawyers. At the federal level, EPA, HHS, IRS, DOC, DOL, SEC, ICE, FCC, DOD, DOE, and many others all have their own in-house lawyers. At the state level, the same thing occurs with lawyers in the state's Department of Commerce, Department of Labor, Department of Transportation, and many others. These lawyers become regulatory experts and legislation advisors in their specific area of the law.

Finally, there are a number of persons who go to law school but, after graduating, never sit for their state bar examination, never get licensed, and never practice as a lawyer. Some of these young men and women grow up knowing their career is going to be in the "family business," whether large or small. Where they graduate in their law school class often does not matter to them because their job with the family business is assured from the start. The J.D. gives them some status and some familiarity with various areas of the law, including labor, tax, regulatory, and corporate, which can help them supervise in-house or outside lawyers the business will need to employ.

Others go to law school to gain the knowledge offered in a law school's business courses (e.g., contracts, administrative law, corporate tax, antitrust, sales, bankruptcy, Uniform Commercial Code, partnerships, transactional law, etc.). These students go to law school to get a J.D. rather than go to business school to get an M.B.A. They want to become entrepreneurs and start their own companies; they don't want to go work for someone else's company. As one fellow student in law school never hesitated to tell me, "I refuse to sell my brains by the hour working for someone else." His view was if you have the "knowledge," you must have the courage to take the "risks" yourself.

In conclusion, the range of legal careers is almost endless, and new areas of practice are continually expanding. For example, there may well be a new need for boutique law firms catering solely to online businesses large and small.

2.3. IT'S NOT ON TV

A major goal of this chapter is to convince you that a legal career is not what you see on TV or in the movies. Many high school students got their initial mental picture of a lawyer from reading *To Kill a Mockingbird* or watching Gregory Peck's moving performance as Atticus Finch in the movie of the same name. Other students watched Joe Pesci in *My Cousin Vinny*; Tom Cruise, Jack Nicholson, and Demi Moore in *A Few Good Men*; Reese Witherspoon in *Legally Blonde*; or Tom Cruise again in *The Firm*. Still other students get their initial images of legal practice from TV shows: "Ally McBeal," "Boston Legal," or "Law and Order." Practicing law for the vast majority of lawyers is not what you see on TV or in the movies. The media glorifies conflict and litigation in the courtroom.

Many lawyers, in private practice and in government, never see the inside of a courtroom. Even in a litigation practice, which I enjoyed for twenty-two years, the vast majority of civil cases settle prior to trial. Most litigators spend days, weeks, and months plowing through documents, seeking to understand the facts of the case and then spend additional days, weeks, and months locating and interviewing witnesses. It is not glamorous work. What follows are often long sessions locating, interviewing, and discussing the facts with potential expert witnesses. Along the way, discovery under the Federal Rules of Civil Procedure takes over with interrogatories, requests for admissions, requests for production of documents, and the taking of depositions, sworn testimony.

The larger the case and the larger the law firm, the less likely a young lawyer will be to earn direct contact with the client much less an opportunity to swear in a witness, take a deposition, or appear in court. It is not unusual for a litigation attorney in his/her third or fourth year in a large or midsize law firm to never have seen the inside of a courtroom, except as a spectator behind the bar. The lesson is simple: do not decide that you want to go to law school because of anything you see on TV or in the movies.

2.4. ASK, INTERVIEW, SHADOW, AND VISIT

The natural question then becomes, how do you find out what a legal career is really like? The answer is that during your first two years of college or university, you must put in time and effort reading as much as you can about the law, the range of legal careers, and what the three years in law school will be like. Your college or university pre-law advisor's office, your career services center, and your library contain more material than you can read in your free time during freshman and sophomore year.

Once you have read substantially, attempt to go and visit lawyers, law firms, law school students, and courtrooms. You will need to find practicing lawyers. This will allow you to talk with them, ask questions, and, if lucky, get permission to shadow them for a day. The place to start to find a practicing lawyer is with your family. If you have a parent, grandparent, sibling, aunt or uncle, cousin, or distant relative who is a lawyer, then you have found a place to start.

Try to speak with that lawyer in person, you will get more information this way. If they live in a distant state, e-mail and ask if you could call and speak with them. During these first interviews, keep it short (thirty minutes or so), follow up on information and questions from what you have read, and be certain you ask both of these questions: "What do you like most about your practice?" and "What do you like least about your practice?" Ask the first lawyer you interview to direct you to one or two other lawyers who might be willing to talk with you. Follow this same procedure.

If you cannot find a family member to start with, ask your parents if they know of a lawyer living in your neighborhood or a legal office not far from where you live. If this second approach does not work, contact your pre-law advisor or the career services center at your college or university and ask if they can direct you to an alum of the school who is a lawyer you could speak to and interview.

Finally, if all else fails, almost all cities, towns, and counties have local bar associations and most of them have a Young Lawyers Section. Go online and get an e-mail address which will allow you to contact the Young Lawyers Section and see if they can arrange an interview for you. A young lawyer out of law school only five years can both answer your questions about their practice and also give you very current information regarding what they experienced for three years as a law school student. Remember to send a sincere "thank you" note either by snail mail or e-mail within two days of each and every interview.

After interviewing, you move on to visits. Remember that federal, state, county, and city courtrooms are public areas. Depending on where you are going to college or university, there will be many opportunities to attend trials and other proceedings, just be certain to dress appropriately and conform with all courtroom decorum. Your pre-law advisor can identify for you whether there is a law school on your campus and, if not, which law schools are closest to your campus. Your pre-law advisor should also be able to put you in touch with a current law school student.

With current law school students, it is the visit and not an interview that is most important. Recognize that law school students continually feel under pressure for time. Respect those pressures and simply ask if you could shadow the student for a morning or an afternoon. Let them pick the most convenient day. In three to five hours, you will begin to develop an idea of the reading load in law school, what a law school class is like, what a law school study session is like, and much more.

Finally, after six months or so, you can recontact one of the lawyers you interviewed and ask if you could shadow them for a day at their firm or office. Summertime, when you are not in classes, is often a great time to attempt to shadow a lawyer. If a date is set, remember to dress professionally. Also remember a shadow stays out of the way. You are there to observe the lawyer you are shadowing and to learn how lawyers spend their day (much of which may be on the phone) and how they interact with one another. You are not there to constantly interrupt or ask questions. Save questions until the end of the day, if at all.

Remember to keep reading about the range of legal careers and law schools while you question, interview, and visit. All of this extra effort can help you decide whether you really have the passion for law school. If, at the end of two years, your GPA is high enough and you are still serious about attending law school, you may wish to try to get a credit or noncredit internship with a law firm, a government agency, or a district attorney's office.

2.5. PRE-LAW PROGRAMS AND ADVISORS

The last three subsections of this chapter are a bit of a digression because they do not relate solely to the first two years of college or university. But it seemed appropriate to flag them for you here. First, almost every college or university has a pre-law program and an official pre-law advisor. Sometimes this individual is a member of the career counseling center. Sometimes this individual is a faculty member in a department that typically sends students on to law school, such as political science, history, or criminal justice. Sometimes this individual can be a former practicing attorney, who upon ceasing practice joined the college or university in an administrative or faculty position. These individuals could be in positions as diverse as assistant deans, the office of university council, or the departments of English, philosophy, accounting, or management.

Wherever the pre-law advisor is housed at your college or university, this is an important resource for you to learn about from the day you first step on campus. These pre-law advisors have books and articles for you to read, websites for you to frequent, knowledge of and contact with prior legal and judicial alums from your institution, and important information about law schools and the law school admissions process. Generally these pre-law ad-visors are members of the The Pre-Law Advisors' National Council (PLANC) or one of its regional sections Northeastern, Southern, Midwest-ern, or Western (NAPLA, SAPLA, MAPLA, or WAPLA). All of these asso-ciations hold annual meetings where members keep abreast of current devel-opments in law school, the law school admissions process, funding law school education, and career options following law school.

A significant part of your mission during freshman and sophomore year is to identify and locate the office of your college or university's pre-law advis-or. Then make an initial appointment to introduce yourself, and continue to make regular visits for the rest of your college or university career to utilize the resources your advisor has available.

2.6. DISCIPLINARY DISCLOSURES

For college and university freshmen interested in going to law school, we already discussed the problems created by a poor academic start (i.e., a low GPA for freshman year which is difficult to raise by the end of junior year). There is a second pitfall for freshmen—disciplinary problems. Every law school application form I look at requires that candidates disclose all crimi-nal convictions and all disciplinary problems on their college or university records. Disciplinary problems come in two varieties—either academic or student affairs.

Of the two, academic problems are by far the most significant. Academic problems would include plagiarism, cheating on examinations, breaking into faculty offices to get an early look at a test, and a good deal more. Every college and university has its own version of an academic integrity policy where "plagiarism" (submitting someone else's work as if it were your own) is at the very heart of the school's policy.

Paying someone in your dorm to write your sociology paper for you is plagiarism. Digging a five-year-old American history paper, which got an A or B+ when it was first submitted, out of a fraternity or sorority file and then resubmitting it as your own work, even with a retyped cover page or even retyped in total, is plagiarism. Ordering your child psychology paper from an online paper mill advertising on a bulletin board in the dorm and submitting that paper as if it were your own is plagiarism. Going on Google or Wikipe-dia and/or multiple other websites to "block copy" paragraphs or pages and then "paste" them into your paper on your computer, submitting them as your ideas, words, and sentences is plagiarism. Plagiarism is considered the most reprehensible academic problem because it is academic dishonesty, academic lying, and academic misrepresentation.

Cheating on exams or quizzes with your iPhone, sending someone else into your class to take an exam in your place, obtaining an unfair advantage over your fellow students through an advance copy of an exam, and lying to academic administrators and/or faculty are also examples of academic dishonesty. Most colleges and universities require that all accusations of plagiarism be submitted to the office of the dean of the school and be investigated. The results of the investigation can end up in the student's permanent academic record.

And there can be post-college repercussions. Generally, the American Bar Association, the fifty separate Committees of State Bar Examiners who must certify a law school graduate's eligibility to sit for the bar exam and thereby obtain a license to practice law, as well as individual law school admissions officers tend to feel that a history of academic dishonesty renders a candidate unfit for law school and/or for legal practice. Any academic disciplinary problems which must be disclosed on law school applications are, therefore, very serious matters.

Student affairs disciplinary matters cover a wider range of infractions and are also serious, but generally they need not be the end to a legal career. Student affairs disciplinary problems can include violations of campus drug and alcohol regulations, run-ins with campus police, rowdiness or destruction of property in dormitories, violations of campus automobile policies, and even off-campus activities occurring at fraternity or sorority houses where the local police are called in and report the students involved to campus security. If the event is on your record, you must disclose it and hopefully you can honestly assert that the regrettable offense happened only once while briefly explaining what you learned and how you grew from the experience.

2.7. QUESTION 1—HOW MUCH WILL IT COST AND HOW DO I PAY FOR IT?

This *Handbook* addresses the "How much will it cost?" and "How will I pay for it?" questions more extensively in chapter 6. But, by the end of sophomore year, students contemplating law school should be thinking about the big financial picture. This picture includes how much the average cost of three years of law school will be in tuition, room, board, books, and so forth, compared to how much the average lawyer graduating from law school will earn during their first few years.

Understand the data provided here are only estimates of averages; the cost of law school education varies widely and the starting salary of newly minted lawyers also varies widely. In March of 2012, the president of PLANC (The Pre-Law Advisors' National Council) released the following figures. Most undergraduates complete their college or university career owing an average of $24,500 in loans that must be repaid. During the twenty years from 1989 to 2009, law school tuition increased almost 320 percent and continues to rise today.

The PLANC article states that in 2009, in-state tuition at public law schools averaged $18,472 per year and private law school tuition averaged $35,743. The "indirect costs"—books, room, board, insurance, and transportation—range between $12,500 and $25,000 per year based on the law schools' own estimates. Therefore, the "cost of attendance" at many of the nation's top law schools now approaches $75,000 per year, or $225,000 over three years. Thus, it is not surprising that the ABA indicates a typical law school student borrows anywhere from $70,000 to $110,000 just to pay for law school. Deferred undergraduate loans, private loans for cars, and credit card debt are not included in this law school debt calculation. You cannot wait until after college graduation to begin considering these costs and how you will repay them.

2.8. QUESTION 2—WHY SUCH HIGH LEVELS OF LAWYER DISSATISFACTION?

Supreme Court Associate Justice Sandra Day O'Connor warned in 2004, "Job dissatisfaction among lawyers is widespread, profound and growing worse." A 2007 American Bar Association (ABA) survey of eight hundred lawyers quickly confirmed Justice O'Connor's warning and revealed the disturbing finding that only four in ten of the lawyers surveyed would recommend a legal career to a young person. This dissatisfaction is a fact undergraduates need to understand before committing to attend law school and incur the debt involved.

What caused this high level of dissatisfaction within the profession? Many lawyers suggest it stems from the current lack of jobs, the long hours, the lack of control over one's schedule, or the difficulty of fitting in time for a personal life. All of these play a part, but Justice O'Connor believes the growing view of lawyers as greedy business men and women out to maximize personal profits raises concern at all levels of the profession. She warned a "win at all costs" mentality means "pushing all the rules of ethics and decency to the limits" and leads to increasing uncivil practices in the law.

In addition, the pressure for billable hours steadily rose at law firms over the past twenty-five years. The impact of rising billable hours caught the attention of former Supreme Court Chief Justice William Rehnquist, who expressed concern that lawyers producing more than two thousand billable hours in a year would be "tempted" to inflate their time. Indeed, as far back as 1996 an article in the *Indiana Law Journal* titled "The Death of an Honorable Profession" raised a series of important questions as to the credibility of some legal billing practices.

Some critics see the rise in billable hours paralleling the transition of the law firm into just another business. Justice O'Connor reminds us that treating the practice of law as a "business" where the "bottom line" is paramount is diametrically opposed to treating the practice of law as a "profession" which recognizes its members have public obligations. For Justice O'Connor, the more lawyers view themselves merely as "hired guns" whose goals are to get well paid for achieving every wish and whim of their client, the more the legal community's commitment to the public good erodes.

By 2009, in the wake of economic scandals, many involving lawyers in business transactions harmful to the public interest, Stephen Gillers, professor of legal ethics at NYU Law School asked a troubling question that underlies this dissatisfaction: "Is law (still) an honorable profession?" I am convinced the law is and can continue to be an honorable profession. I continue to encourage many of my best students to consider a career in law. But the two faces of the law, one driven by money and one driven by service, remain real, and undergraduates interested in attending law school need to know that reality.

Chapter Three

The Time Table Junior Year

3.1. COUNTING BACKWARD

For undergraduates planning to attend law school, junior year is the most critical year. To properly understand what must be done junior year, you need to understand when all your law school applications must be completed and submitted as well as what needs to be accomplished before those submissions can happen. Many undergraduates are unintentionally misled by law school websites on this critical timing issue. Law school applications are submitted online with backup documentation (transcripts, LSAT scores, letters of recommendation, resumes) also submitted electronically through Law School Admission Council (LSAC), discussed in chapter 7.

Application forms do not become "live" or available to be worked on until late in August or early September of your senior year. The law school websites variously inform you that they will consider your application up to the end of February or March, some even later. This is true; but those same websites tell you that the law school uses a "rolling admissions" policy. That is, the law school admissions officers begin reviewing applications and making decisions on "acceptance" or "rejection" in late November or early December.

I encourage my students and pre-law advisees to develop a schedule that allows them to submit all their law school applications before they head home for Thanksgiving senior year. Why place this pressure on seniors when the law school websites announce that candidates can submit their applications as late as March? To answer this question, you must understand the small size of law school classes and the high level of competition for seats in first year classes.

Compared to undergraduate freshman class size, most law schools enroll very small first year classes, perhaps 150 to 300 students in a law school's 1L class. As with all schools, law schools must "admit" more students than they know will "matriculate" in order to be certain their first year class is filled.

If we take the state of Massachusetts as an example, there are seven ABA-accredited law schools within the state. And during one year, these seven law schools received from a low of 1,317 applications to a high of 8,515 applications each and matriculated first-year classes that ranged in size from a low of 133 students to a high of 561 students. There is no one acceptance formula that applies to all law schools, but there is stiff competition for admission at all law schools.

For example, in alphabetical order in Massachusetts:

Boston College	6,873 applications	20 percent of applicants accepted
	1,359 acceptances	19 percent of accepted matriculate
	261 matriculated	4 percent of applicants matriculate
Boston University	8,515 applications	20 percent of applicants accepted
	1,747 acceptances	15 percent of accepted matriculate
	268 matriculated	3 percent of applicants matriculate
Harvard University	7,574 applications	11 percent of applicants accepted
	833 acceptances	67 percent of accepted matriculate
	561 matriculated	7 percent of applicants matriculate
New England Law Boston	2,734 applications	61 percent of applicants accepted
	1,680 acceptances	21 percent of accepted matriculate
	361 matriculated	13 percent of applicants matriculate

Northeastern	4,311 applications	31 percent of applicants accepted
	1,360 acceptances	16 percent of accepted matriculate
	220 matriculated	5 percent of applicants matriculate
Suffolk	2,727 applications	53 percent of applicants accepted
	1,459 acceptances	23 percent of accepted matriculate
	328 matriculated	12 percent of applicants matriculate
Western New England	1,317 applications	53 percent of applicants accepted
	699 acceptances	19 percent of accepted matriculate
	133 matriculated	10 percent of applicants matriculate

Obviously, Harvard Law School with a 1L class size of 560 is the exception, with the remaining six schools having a 1L class size of 133 to 361. Also note that only 4 percent to 13 percent of the total applicants ever matriculate at all seven schools.

Law schools make a great deal of money for their institutions, whether public or private. Most law schools teach their 1L classes in large sections of one hundred to two hundred students, don't need as many faculty as undergraduate institutions, require less financing for laboratories and equipment than disciplines in science, medicine, or engineering, and still charge yearly tuition in the $45,000 plus range.

Assume a law school is charging $50,000 per year in tuition and wants a 1L class of two hundred, but the dean of admissions miscalculates the number of students who need to be "admitted" to result in a 1L class of two hundred who actually "matriculate" and pay tuition. Assume further the dean misses by only five students and so enrolls only 195 tuition-paying students; that sounds pretty good. But note, those five students lose the institution $250,000 in tuition the first year and $750,000, or three-quarters of a million dollars, over three years.

Human nature being what it is, I believe that psychologically law school admissions officers read applications with a more open attitude in December when they know they must fill every one of their two hundred 1L seats or risk losing money than they read an identical application in February, March, and even April. In those later months, when the law school already accepted eight hundred students for its two hundred 1L seats and believes it is very close to, if not over, having its 1L class totally filled, applications that present close calls are easier to "reject" than they are in December when every one of the two hundred 1L seats still need to be filled.

3.2. THE FRIDAY BEFORE THANKSGIVING

For these reasons, I encourage my students and advisees to complete and submit all of their law school applications before they go home for the Thanksgiving holiday in November of senior year. Once this target date is set, all that is needed is to "count backward" and decide when all of the tasks leading up to a completed application must be done. These tasks include:

- When do I prepare for the LSAT?
- When do I take the LSAT?
- When do I open an LSAC account?
- When do I get my official transcript(s)?
- When do I prepare my resume?
- When do I get my letters of recommendation?
- When do I write my personal statement?

3.3. TEST PREP, TEST PREP, AND MORE TEST PREP

The key to and most critical component of your application is your score on the Law School Admission Test (LSAT), discussed in greater detail in chapter 4. The LSAT is not like the SAT, which tests your basic math and verbal skills. The LSAT is not like the MCAT, which tests your knowledge in chemistry, biology, and mathematics; nor like the GRE, which tests your knowledge in a specific discipline like history, English, or political science. The LSAT tests your logical reasoning ability; it tests nothing factual that you learned in high school or as an undergraduate. If, while taking the LSAT, you believe that something you learned in your history, business law, anthropology, or criminal justice class gives you a right answer, I guarantee you are being tricked into the wrong answer.

Just because you have a 3.9 or 4.0 GPA doesn't mean you are ready for the LSAT. The specifics of LSAT questions change from year to year, but the nature of the questions remains constant. Thus you can learn to understand the nature of the questions and the modes of reasoning being tested. This means that, whatever your GPA, you can learn to maximize your score on the LSAT and, thereby, maximize your chance for law school admission. However, to do this requires practice and practice and more practice with official prior LSAT examinations.

Based on multiple interviews with my students and pre-law advisees, I am confident that 250–300 hours of intensive practice with official prior LSAT examinations is the "minimum" amount of practice time required for students to maximize their score. I understand that the T.R.I.A.L.S. Program run in alternate summers at Harvard and NYU law schools instructs their students that five hundred hours of practice is the minimum.

Step one in counting backward from the application submission deadline of Thanksgiving in senior year, then, is to decide when you will have the time to put in this 250–300 hours of intensive study for the LSAT.

3.4. TIMING OF THE LSAT

In making this decision on when you will do the preparation, you must understand that the LSAT is administered in all fifty states on the same day only four times during the year—in June, in late September or early October, in December, and in February. For example, during the 2012–2013 academic year, the LSAT is offered on Monday June 11, Saturday October 6, Saturday December 1, and Saturday February 9. Your LSAT score will be sent to you electronically three weeks after the completion of the test. For the June test, this means you will know your score before July 4; for the October test, by November 1; for the December test, shortly after Christmas; and for the February test, in early March. Only the June test in the summer after junior year or the October test in senior year allow you to have all law school applications submitted by Thanksgiving of senior year.

While you may have identified law schools you would "like" to go to or "hope" to apply to or "want" to attend, the reality is you cannot know "where" or even "if" your application will be competitive unless and until you have your LSAT score. Only then can you begin the process of considering and selecting law schools where your application will be either "competitive" (a 1L class composed of persons with approximately your LSAT score and your GPA) or "safe" (a 1L class composed of persons with LSAT scores and GPAs below your LSAT score and GPA).

On occasion, even excellent students do not perform as well as they wanted to on the LSAT. And, it is not unusual for solid students (in the B range) to badly underperform on the LSAT, especially if they scrimped on their practice time. Thus, even the October LSAT can place a great deal of pressure on senior undergraduates. You cannot begin to seriously know where you should send your applications until approximately November 1, when you know your score. At that point, if the score is not what you were hoping for, you may need to be rethinking your law school goals from where you would "like" to go, which may now be out of the question, to where you can be "admitted."

3.5. LSAC ACCOUNTS

Registration to take the LSAT examination anywhere in the country can be accomplished electronically, in writing, or over the phone through the Law School Admission Council (LSAC) in Newtown, Pennsylvania. As discussed further in chapter 7, at the time students register to take the LSAT, most undergraduates open their account with LSAC. After you open your account, LSAC preserves your LSAT score and every document you submit to them in your private account with your particular account number and your unique bar code. Your undergraduate transcript(s), your letters of recommendation, and your personal statement are all stored and preserved in your LSAC account, which only you can access online with your account number. This way, you can check online to be certain the official transcripts you ordered from the registrar's office at each undergraduate institution you attended, each letter of recommendation a professor agreed to write for you, as well as your personal statement are all received by LSAC and placed in your account.

3.6. LETTERS OF RECOMMENDATION

Law school admissions applications generally ask for two or three letters of recommendation. With letters of recommendation, there are basically two key questions for you to consider:

- Who should you ask to write the recommendation? and
- What should the letter say to advance your application?

The point to remember here is that these are letters of recommendation to law "school" and not to the practice of law. There are certain basic skills that law schools want the members of their incoming 1L class to possess. Among those skills are (1) the ability to critically read and retain vast amounts of material, (2) the ability to analyze arguments logically and carefully, (3) the ability to view facts and situations from multiple perspectives, and (4) the ability to distinguish and differentiate facts and situations. The ABA website states that most law schools are looking for a specific set of skills that will lead to success in law school.

These include **analytical and problem-solving skills**, **critical reading** abilities, **writing** skills, **oral communication** and listening abilities, general **research** skills, task **organization and management** skills, and the values of serving faithfully the interests of others while also promoting justice. (emphasis added)

The people in your life who can address these skills most directly will be undergraduate faculty members and in some cases immediate work supervisors. Family friends, politicians, and alumni of a particular law school can also all write letters of recommendation, but they don't know you personally and cannot identify the classroom skills the law school is seeking.

In reviewing letters of recommendation, law school admissions officers acknowledge they are looking for specific and detailed facts demonstrating that a student possesses these skills to excel at their law school. For law school letters of recommendation, facts about a candidate's skills are the highest form of advocacy. Identifying the *specific paper, oral presentation, or examination* where the student excelled will set him/her apart from the thousands of other applicants. Identifying the *specific research project* where the student's insight, creativity, and analytical skills amazed and delighted a faculty member will make the letter memorable.

The volume of letters of recommendation nationwide each year is overwhelming. For the first-year law school class of 2011, a few examples from the ABA-LSAC data highlight the issue. For the University of Maine Law School, there were approximately 1,300 applicants or 2,600 letters of recommendation for 95 1L seats, for Villanova University School of Law outside Philadelphia there were 3,700 applicants or 7,400 letters for 251 1L seats, for the University of North Carolina Law School there were 3,100 applicants or 6,200 letters for 254 1L seats, for Duke University Law School there were 7,900 applicants or 15,800 letters for 238 1L seats, for the University of Illinois Law School there were 4,800 applicants or 9,600 letters for 224 1L seats, for the University of Chicago Law School there were 5,600 applicants or 11,200 letters for 205 1L seats, and for the University of California Berkeley Law School there were 8,300 applicants or 16,600 letters for 286 1L seats.

With each law school receiving somewhere between 2,600 and 16,600 letters of recommendation each year, the faculty writing your letters of recommendation need to recognize how frequently the terms "excellent," "great," "outstanding," "the best," "superior," "gifted," "very talented," along with a thousand other accolades, appear in these letters of recommendation. You need to ask yourself, if you were a member of the law school admissions staff reviewing applicant files, how would you or could you

possibly assess highly generic letters of recommendation? The fact is gener-
alities cannot help you; only "specific data" can potentially impact a decision
to accept an applicant.

For many years, I have believed letters of recommendation generally
cannot get a candidate "accepted" but can help get a candidate "rejected"
from a law school. A bland, short, perfunctory letter can push that file closer
to the "reject" pile. I wrote hundreds of letters of recommendation to law
schools in my twenty-three years of university teaching and my twenty-two
years of legal practice. I believe I know how to write a detailed and specific
letter of recommendation that will not hurt an applicant. But, the only times I
believe my letter of recommendation truly helped an applicant gain acceptance are in those few instances when I can state in my letter "three years
ago, I recommended so-and-so to you, you accepted him/her, and she/he is
now graduating at the top of your class as executive editor of your law
review." If I can then honestly state "the student I am recommending today is
just as good and, perhaps, better than the executive editor of your law review
was as an undergraduate," then and only then do I think my letter truly makes
a difference.

Applicants to law school need to help out the faculty members who will
ultimately write the letters of recommendation for them. From freshman year
on, pre-law students, as noted, need to preserve their A papers, the positive
faculty comments on projects and presentations, and the occasional A+ on a
midterm exam. Faculty simply cannot be expected to remember the specifics.
And the larger the college or university or the larger the class size, the less
likely any professor can remember your specifics from a year or two years
ago. However, if you can preserve these materials and provide them to your
recommender, the letters of recommendation will be more detailed, more
specific, and less likely to hurt you.

Always ask a faculty member in person, face-to-face, to write a letter of
recommendation for you. If you ask and you do not get a positive and
enthusiastic response, you asked the wrong person. If the faculty member
says, "well, isn't there someone who knows you better than I do," what kind
of letter can you expect? You do not want a mediocre letter that pushes your
application closer to the reject pile. By the beginning or middle of junior
year, you should develop a fairly good idea of the two or three faculty
members you will be asking to write your letters of recommendation.

3.7. RESUMES

You will need a resume to apply to law school. Junior year is the time to
prepare a resume if you do not already have one. I encourage my students to
start building their resume when they start building their GPA—in freshman

year. Join clubs and activities you enjoy so that by junior year you hold leadership positions. If a service activity is attractive to you, do it. Joining the pre-law society, moot court, and mock trial at the start of senior year to build your resume is transparent and unhelpful. You are better off to be in student government, or the College Democrats, or the Appalachian Project from freshman or sophomore year forward.

You are building a resume for law school, not for employment. Do not let career services tell you to place a "goal" at the top of the resume; the law schools know that every applicant's goal is the same: to gain acceptance. And do not place any high school information, including where you went to high school, on the resume; law schools do not care that in high school you were senior class president, cocaptain of the basketball team, won your community's citizenship essay contest, or have trophies from statewide mock trial competitions.

The only exception I make is when students attended high school outside the country. If one of your parents serves in the military or is in the Foreign Service and you went to high school in Germany, or Dubai, or the Netherlands, then list the high school, city, and country. Law schools will find that information an interesting diversity factor.

I encourage students to build a one-page resume with five basic headings (1) Personal Information, (2) Education, (3) Honors and Awards, (4) Experience, (5) Activities, Leadership, Service, and perhaps a sixth, (6) Personal Interests. Each of these headings will be discussed in detail in chapter 7 on the application process.

3.8. PERSONAL STATEMENTS

Many undergraduates find writing their personal statement one of the great stumbling blocks of the law school application process, discussed in more detail in chapter 7. For now, it is enough to point out that taking your LSAT in June after your junior year allows you to get your LSAT score by July 1. That score, along with your GPA for your first three years, allows you to begin to winnow down the law schools at which your credentials may be competitive and to which you may want to apply. Therefore, you can begin thinking seriously in July and August, when you are not burdened with classes, papers, and senior year activities, about what you could write for your personal essay.

Writing about yourself is not easy; it takes time and it takes thought. What event, experience, or moment made you certain you would go to law school? What difficulty, pain, or burden did you overcome in your life that makes you know you could handle law school? What is your great passion or your great gift? Who are you as a person entering senior year?

Plan this essay to be about two and one-half pages double-spaced. One page is not enough; five pages is probably way too long. You are applying to a professional school that teaches above all else "advocacy." Your personal essay is your one and only chance in the application process to "advocate" for yourself. At the start of senior year, you cannot change your GPA or your LSAT score if you took it in June. And you cannot dramatically change your resume. Joining fifteen clubs and activities at the start of senior year when you were a wallflower for the first three years or locked in your room playing video games will not fix three years of inactivity.

But, in the two and one-half pages of your personal statement, you can disclose the best of you, the uniqueness of you. Do not write about yourself in the future, how you will change the profession or become a famous jurist. Those are your dreams, that is not you right now. Write about what is best in you and lead the law school faculty member reading your file to conclude, "I would like to have this man or this woman in my class." This is your chance to advocate for you. Depending on the schools where you are applying, each admissions office is receiving and reading three thousand to six thousand or more personal statements. You can and must find a way to stand out.

Some law schools just ask for a single generic personal statement. Other law schools require that your essay also address why you are a "good fit" for their particular law school. Still other law schools will ask for both a personal statement and a second essay on a particular question or issue posed on that school's application.

Your personal essay, and any other required essay, must be letter-perfect—no typos, no spelling, diction, capitalization, or grammar errors are allowed. You are seeking to join a profession; keep it professional—no fancy script, and no colored paper. You are not trying out for a sports team, a dance team, or a circus—no videotapes, no CDs.

There are plenty of web-based paper mills offering to write personal statements for law school candidates at a price. Most charge substantial fees. None of them know you or care about you. Don't even think about it.

You must own your personal statement. There is a great one in each and every one of you. You simply have to find it. Your best friend cannot write it for you, although I hope she/he will listen to it, read it, and give you an honest reaction to it. Your English teacher and your pre-law advisor cannot write it for you either. Again, I hope someone you trust on the faculty will read a draft and highlight any problems with sentence structure, diction, spelling, grammar, and the rest.

Personally, I learned a technique for personal statements, which I use to this day, from another pre-law advisor. Each time a student comes to my office with their personal essay in hand and asks if they could leave it with me so I could read it, I say, "no." I then insist that they sit down with me right then and place the paper facedown on the desk so that neither he/she nor I can see it. I then ask the student to tell me in two simple sentences what the "take away" message from their personal essay is. When they cannot tell me, I hand the personal essay back still unread. I ask them to figure out what that "take away" message is and to make certain that their message is at the front of the opening paragraph, reiterated in different words in the final paragraph, and proven in the body of the personal essay.

3.9. WAITING FOR A YEAR OR TWO

A growing number of undergraduate students decide to defer their application to law school for a year or two or even more. The reasons for this decision to defer vary widely. Some students want to pay down their outstanding undergraduate school debt before going deeper into debt; others are still not certain if a legal career is what they really desire. Some students knew they were not ready and prepared for the LSAT; while others believed they were prepared, but were not, and after getting their scores wisely decided not to apply. Still other students don't want to go from four years of reading, study, and testing, straight into three more years of even more intensive reading, study, and testing. Some of these students defer simply to take a year to travel the country with a friend, backpack across Europe, or volunteer at Vista, Teach America, or City Year.

Law school admissions counselors appear to look favorably at such deferrals. Admissions officers are always wary of those undergraduates who decide to go to law school by default. Some students who do not like or cannot handle math and science and so are not in pre-med, and who are not attracted to banking or accounting and so will not pursue an M.B.A., but who love reading and are excellent students in English, history, philosophy, or political science, apply to law school by default. These students typically liked school, performed well (especially on standardized examinations), but found no burning career path driving them. By late junior year, under recurring questioning from parents, relatives, friends, and even teachers asking, "What are you going to do after graduation?" many of these students find it easier to simply say they are going to law school than to continue to say, "Honestly, I have no idea."

Of the students who attend law school by default, some succeed and go on to long legal careers, while others drop out. Both law school admissions officers and undergraduate pre-law advisors know that the last place we want a student learning that law school is really not for him/her is during the first year of law school. When this happens, as it does every year, both the law school admissions process and the pre-law advisor likely failed that student. So it is "OK" to defer for a year or two until you become certain law school is for you.

Indeed, taking a year to travel, to volunteer, to learn something new, to just follow your passion creates very positive and interesting impacts on your resume when you do apply. Your experiences walking the Appalachian Trail, or teaching children in a rural community in Louisiana or an Indian village in Arizona, or organizing projects for City Year in Baltimore will surely set you apart from the thousands of undergraduates applying straight from college. Your experience working in a state legislator's office or traveling in Australia may provide the perfect backdrop for a personal statement that truly reveals who you are as a person and what you can bring to a law school community.

Chapter Four

The LSAT

This *Handbook* tries, multiple times, to reinforce the understanding that the most important part of your law school application is your LSAT score. Law school admissions officers will tell you that the admissions process considers "everything": grades, courses, letters of recommendation, personal statement, undergraduate institution, activities and leadership, resume, absolutely everything, including the LSAT score.

I am certain that everything in each candidate's file is reviewed and considered. But the real question is how much weight each item is given? I remain confident that in considering "everything," the LSAT score carries the most weight. The law schools themselves admit the LSAT score is their best predictor of success in the first year of law school. Moreover, law school rankings are heavily influenced by the incoming students' LSAT scores and GPAs. But the data I collected makes it clear that the LSAT score typically counts more than the GPA.

I have seen gifted students with excellent GPAs, 3.85 or 3.77 for example, who cannot get accepted at any first-, second-, or third-tier law school because they scored 147 and 148 respectively on the LSAT. Indeed, students scoring in the mid-140s will find a very small pool of low-ranked law schools where their credentials will be competitive or even viable. On the other hand, I have seen mediocre students with mediocre GPAs gain admission into top one hundred law schools apparently because of their LSAT scores—2.38 GPA but 161 LSAT, 2.69 GPA but 159 LSAT, 2.77 GPA but 168 LSAT, for example. None of these students brought racial or ethnic diversity to the schools in question.

To be clear, this is not from national data. The only data I possess comes from LSAT scores and GPAs for undergraduate students at my home institution where I serve as the pre-law advisor. And I only possess this data for a limited number of years: 1999 through 2011. The data comes from the annual *LSAC Action Reports* prepared and released around February of each year and covers the actions taken ("accept," "matriculate," "withdrawal," and "other," i.e., reject) with regard to the students applying the year before. Students entering law school in August of 2011 would appear in the *February 2012 Action Report.*

Based upon the experience of my students and advisees, the LSAT score carries the most weight in the candidate's application package and the GPA combined with the reputation of the undergraduate institution carries the second most weight.

The LSAT is taken by approximately 150,000 students who have previously graduated from or are graduating from college or university each year. Competition is strong. Three weeks after taking the LSAT, you will receive an e-mail with your scores. You will receive both a "raw" score and a "scaled" score. Your "raw" score is the actual number of right answers out of the approximately one hundred multiple choice questions on the four scored sections of the test. Unlike the SAT, the LSAT does not take points off for wrong answers, so you never leave an answer blank. There is no penalty for blind guessing.

Your scaled score will range from a potential low of 120 and a percentile ranking of 0.0 percent for fifteen or fewer correct answers to a high of 180 and a percentile ranking of 99.9 percent for ninety-nine to one hundred right answers. But note that every scaled score from 173 to 180 (approximately ninety-five right answers and above) is in the ninety-ninth percentile.

I ask my own students to set an initial goal when they first start preparing for the LSAT of a scaled score of "at least" 155, or approximately sixty-nine to seventy right answers, for a percentile ranking of 63.7 percent. The second goal is to obtain a scaled score of 160, which requires about seventy-nine right answers and provides a percentile ranking of 80 percent. The third goal is a scaled score of 165, which places you into the ninety-first percentile and makes you competitive at all but the most elite law schools.

4.1. PREP COURSES—DO I NEED ONE?

Most students discover that they need a prep course prior to taking the LSAT. The LSAT, like the SAT for admission to college, the MCAT for admission to medical school, or the GRE for admission to graduate school, is a nationally standardized test. However, unlike the other nationally standardized tests, the LSAT does not test facts, knowledge, or learned information. The LSAT tests only logic, reasoning, and reading skills under time pressure. Unlike the other standardized tests, the LSAT also intentionally attempts to mislead students into selecting incorrect answers, in other words, "attractive distracters."

Given the unique nature of this LSAT examination, most students decide they need a prep course, at a bare minimum, to get a better handle on the three types of multiple choice questions and the various tricks imbedded in every test. Many commercial vendors offer LSAT preparation courses from Princeton Review, to PowerScore, TestMasters, Blueprint, Kaplan, ExamKrackers, and a number of others. The cost of these commercial programs can range up to $2,000. In addition, there are some two- or three-day weekend courses that introduce you to the nature of the questions on the LSAT and then leave you to practice on your own. Some colleges and universities even offer noncredit courses to prepare their students for the exam.

4.2. TEST DAY—IT'S NOT AS SHORT AS YOU THINK

Despite the fact that the LSAT score is calculated from only four multiple choice tests of approximately twenty-five points each, and lasting thirty-five minutes each, the LSAT is also a physically and emotionally grueling test. You are told to be at the test center no later than 8:30; some students start arriving as early as 7:45 under the mistaken belief that the test will "start" at 8:30, last only two hours and twenty minutes, and be over by 11:00. It is not that short.

And many test takers refuse to believe the instructions on the LSAC website and their own admission ticket that many items, some of which students feel they cannot live without, are prohibited at the exam site. Prohibited items include cell phones, BlackBerrys, iPads, mechanical pencils, digital watches, timers of any kind, purses, backpacks, and more. Numerous test takers arriving at the test site with these forbidden items are flustered at having to run back to the car to lock them up, having them confiscated, or being barred from the test.

Sign-in and security procedures for the test are lengthy, including a current photograph, checking signatures, checking IDs, thumb printing, and seat assignment. Test booklets must be distributed and paperwork completed prior to the start of the test; this includes the written identification of which student receives which test booklet by code number. Proctors must clearly read out loud both the instructions for filling in the paperwork and the specific instructions for the first thirty-five-minute test. At a test center handling one hundred, two hundred, or more students, the first section of the LSAT can easily not start until 9:15 or 9:30.

And there are not just four thirty-five-minute tests, there are a total of six thirty-five-minute tests. There is a fifth twenty-five-point multiple choice test that will not affect your grade or become part of your LSAT score but is being used to help standardize future test questions for future exams. This multiple choice section is not identified in any way as ungraded so you expend the same degree of intense effort and concentration on that section as on all of the sections. And there is a final sixth writing sample section at the very end of the text. Thus, all six thirty-five-minute test sections actually total three and a half hours. There is also a bathroom and snack break between test sections three and four for roughly fifteen minutes.

More time will be consumed by this break since all test materials must be collected prior to the break and the right test materials must be returned to the right student after the break. The total testing process can easily exceed four hours. Assuming you start the test at 9:15, you may have your test materials collected and be dismissed from the test at 1:30. But depending on how efficient your room supervisor and proctors are, this dismissal time could easily be after 2:00. Assume you arrived at 7:45, this process amounts to over six hours of constant pressure and the feeling of competition. This explains why the LSAT is both a physically and emotionally grueling examination.

Many students who practice for the LSAT only by taking individual sections of twenty-five questions each and then reviewing their right and wrong answers tend to overestimate how they will perform on a full-length test. Some of them even run out of energy on the day of the official exam. It is good practice to take a number of full-scale practice tests with officially released LSAT exams under actual test conditions prior to sitting for the official LSAT.

4.3. THE NATURE OF THE QUESTIONS

Each LSAT exam contains three types of multiple choice questions. Most sections contain twenty-five questions each which must be completed in thirty-five minutes, leaving you only one minute and twenty-four seconds for each question. And this does not include the time required to read and understand the question or reading passage at issue. As noted previously, there are four total scored multiple choice sections giving you a potential of one hundred right answers. To add to your stress, the fifth multiple choice section, which will not be graded or counted as part of your raw or scaled score, nonetheless demands that you exert just as much effort and energy every one minute and twenty-four seconds on that section as on the sections that really do count.

This test is unlike anything you have taken before and unlike anything you will take later. No facts you learned will be tested on this exam. Moreover, the exam is intentionally constructed to mislead you with what some LSAT prep courses refer to as "attractive distracters"—answers that, especially under the time pressure, look like they may be right and cause you to jump to them.

    a. *Reading Comprehension*: This section seeks to measure your ability to read and understand complex and lengthy passages in a very limited period of time. The reading comprehension sections often contain four passages, some could contain five, with each passage followed by five to eight questions testing your reading and reasoning skills. These passages can come from any discipline, from cell biology, to anthropology, to impressionist art, or economic theory. Keep in mind these questions are not testing facts you learned in college or in high school. Everything you need is in the reading passage and what can be reasoned from the passage. But a warning—most of these passages are fairly long, fifty-five to sixty-five lines, approximately five hundred to six hundred words, in many cases. And they are followed by five to eight questions each with five potential answers. Moreover, the test directions warn you that more than one potential answer "could conceivably answer the question" and that your task is to choose "the *best* answer" that "most accurately and completely answers the question."

In addition to carefully studying the questions in the reading comprehension sections on former official LSAT examinations, undergraduates can improve their reading skills by selecting undergraduate elective courses that require a substantial amount of reading in a wide range of academic areas from history, to comparative literature, to anthropology, to philosophy of science. In addition, undergraduates can swim against the current trend to search out all information electronically and develop the habit of reading for personal enjoyment every week, whether that reading is biography, mystery, essays, or fiction. Lawyers by and large read for a living; it is not too early for you to start.

    b. *Analytical Reasoning*: This section of the LSAT seeks to measure your ability to understand complex structures and to draw logical conclusions. These questions ask you to reason deductively from statements, rules, or principles governing a relationship among people, things, or events. Fondly called by test takers the "logic games" section, this section will ask you based on only partial information to reason out anything from the proper seating order at a dinner party to the identification of which fish can survive with each other in five separate aquariums. While most students just beginning their preparation for the LSAT find this the most daunting section on the test, it is not. There actually are a limited number of logic games. Once you take a sufficient number of practice tests, you should reach the point where upon reading the problem you can say "oh, it's that kind of a game—all I have to do is draw it up this way and the pieces will fall into place." Generally, the analytical reasoning section has only twenty-three or so total questions. By the end of 250 to 300 hours of study, good candidates for law school who put in the right amount of preparation ought to be getting nineteen correct out of twenty-three in this section on every practice test. The following is a piece of a logic game from the September 2006 Official LSAT:

A child eating alphabet soup notices that the only letters left in her bowl are one each of these six letters: T, U, W, X, Y, and Z. She plays a game with the remaining letters, eating them in the next three spoonfuls in accord with certain rules. Each of the letters must be in exactly one of the next three spoonfuls, and each of the spoonfuls must have at least one and at most three letters. In addition, she obeys the following restrictions:

The U is in a later spoonful than the T.
The U is not in a later spoonful than the X.
The Y is in a later spoonful than the W.
The U is in the same spoonful as either the Y or the X but not both.

The fifth question in this logic game section then asks, If the T is in the second spoonful, then which one of the following could be true?

    a. Exactly two letters are in the first spoonful.
    b. Exactly three letters are in the first spoonful.
    c. Exactly three letters are in the second spoonful
    d. Exactly one letter is in the third spoonful.
    e. Exactly two letters are in the third spoonful.

For many undergraduates, learning how to tackle and diagram these analytical reasoning or logic games problems makes the price of commercial LSAT preparation courses well worth the cost.

c. *Logical Reasoning*: This section seeks to measure your critical thinking ability. It provides short passages to read and then asks one or two questions about the passage. You will be asked to draw conclusions, to determine how additional evidence or conflicting evidence would change an argument, to reason by analogy, and to identify flaws in arguments. Philosophy departments at many colleges and universities offer courses in either formal logic or in critical thinking where the college textbook actually addresses logical flaws or fallacies. In some instances, these textbooks even utilize some of the questions from previously released LSAT examinations as problems in the course.

In addition to studying the logical reasoning questions on prior official LSAT examinations, some students find the following useful. Find a classmate who is also studying for the LSAT. Each day take ten minutes or more to read Op-Ed columns in *The New York Times*, *The Wall Street Journal*, or *The Financial Times*. These Op-Eds are heavily devoted to policy advocacy on economics, foreign policy, and social issues. Then together discuss what additional facts, evidence, or arguments the author could add to strengthen the argument as well as what facts, evidence, or arguments are not in the article but which could weaken or even contradict the author's position.

4.4. HOW MUCH PREPARATION IS ENOUGH?

The preparation will vary for each person. Each person is different in his/her ability to study, concentrate, and retain. All I can tell you is that I have interviewed every student over the past five years from my institution who received a scaled score on the LSAT of 160 or better, that is roughly the eightieth percentile or better. And every one of them told me that in addition to whatever prep course they took, they put in over 250 hours, sometimes over 300 hours, of intensive study. This includes taking full-scale practice tests with officially released LSAT exams.

One of the most respected LSAT preparation programs in the country, administered at Harvard and NYU law schools, asserts that five hundred hours of intensive prep combined with practice on every single officially released LSAT exam is required to master the test.

While you can learn to improve your score on this test, the reality is that not everyone can get to 170 or even to 160. There will come a point at which your scores on the officially released LSAT exams you are practicing will reach a plateau. Every time you take a new practice exam, you get the same 156 or 157. Nothing you do seems to improve upon that scaled score. Maybe its time to simply bite the bullet and take the test, acknowledging there are a good number of solid law schools where your 156 or 157 will be competitive for admission.

4.5. BUT, CAN'T I TAKE IT AGAIN?

Yes, if you are unhappy with your LSAT score, you can take the LSAT a second time or even a third time. But, ideally you want to take this test once and only once and not until you feel you are fully prepared. The vast majority of test takers sit for the LSAT only once. Only about 25 percent take the LSAT a second time.

Moreover, if you take the LSAT a second time, the law schools you are applying to will see *all* of your LSAT scores. Many test takers who sit for the LSAT a second time seem confused about what score really "counts" when you send in an application and have two test scores. The source of this confusion arose in 2010 when the ABA instructed all of its accredited law schools to submit their yearly data on matriculated applicants, including the applicant's LSAT scores, using only the applicant's "highest score."

This does not mean the law school only considers your highest score. Historically, law schools tended to average scores. So hypothetically a first score of only 149 (approximately fifty-seven correct answers out of one hundred and a percentile of 40.3 percent) and a second improved score six months later of 156 (approximately seventy-one correct answers and a percentile of 66.9 percent) may well be viewed by the law school as a composite of 152 or 153 with a still borderline percentile of only 51.2 percent. In addition, law schools become suspicious of major increases in LSAT scores, especially when two exams are taken in the same year.

Moreover, there is a real risk in taking the LSAT a second time. Retaking the LSAT, even after putting in additional concentrated preparation, does not assure you of a higher score. Using LSAC's data from the 2010–2011 test, 1,804 test takers with scaled scores of 143 retook the LSAT. Of those retests, 689 or almost 40 percent either made no improvement or actually received lower scores on the second test. Of the 1,215 who improved their score, the standard deviation was only 4.8 points. Indeed, the average LSAT score for all 1,804 retests with original scores of 143 was only 145.6. Given this background data, you can understand why law schools would be very skeptical about an increase in a scaled score from 149 to 158, for example. The truth is it just is not supposed to happen.

The lesson here is not to take the test a second or a third time but to be fully prepared before you take it the first time.

4.6. WHAT TO KNOW ABOUT THE SCORES

As noted previously, you actually get two scores on the LSAT. Your "raw" score is based on one hundred multiple choice questions on the four scored sections discussed earlier. You can pay LSAC for a breakdown which identifies precisely which questions you got right and wrong to produce your raw score. You also get a "scaled" score on a scale running from a low of 120 to a high of 180. Thus the one hundred possible correct answers comprising your "raw" score get "translated" into a more compressed sixty-point "scaled" score.

This translation or compression process pushes the great mass of test takers into the middle of the scaled score and the percentile rankings. For example, 50 out of 100 correct answers results in a scaled score of 145 and a percentile of only 26.3 percent. Ten additional correct answers will get you to a raw score of 59 or 60, which produces a scaled score of 150 and a percentile jump to 44.2 percent. Just three more correct answers pushes you to a raw score of 63, a scaled score of 152, and a further percentile jump to 51.7 percent, moving you into the top half of all test takers.

At this point, little increases in raw score (only one, two, or three additional correct answers) can produce big impacts on scaled scores in the 150 and 160 range and on percentile rankings. A raw score of 70 correct answers gets you a scaled score of 155 and a percentile ranking of 63.7 percent. A raw score of 78 correct answers (a C grade in most college courses) gets you a scaled score of 160 and a percentile ranking of 79.9 percent. You are now in the top 20 percent of all test takers. A raw score of 86 correct answers (a standard B in most college courses) gets you a scaled score of 165 and a percentile of 91.5 percent, and now you can begin to look at some tier-one schools.

This forced clustering in the middle is why I encourage students to set as their initial target a scaled score of 155 while taking practice tests. But the real goal is to achieve a scaled score of 160 where you are in the top 20 percent of test takers and assured of getting into a good law school.

4.7. THE NIGHT AFTER THE TEST

To help you deal with the daylong pressure of this test, in the weeks and months of study beforehand make plans for a night out with your friends. Pick the place and the people you will be comfortable and at ease with for the evening. If two or three of your friends are taking the LSAT that same day, it is fine to make it a group night out. You all deserve it. BUT there is one rule. Once the last section of the exam, the writing sample, is collected, and you walk out of the room, do not talk about the test—not with the other test takers who suffered through the six sections with you, not with your roommate, not with your soul mate. Talking about the test and especially about specific questions on the test can change nothing and can drive you crazy. So just go out, forget it, and have fun. You earned it.

Chapter Five

Choosing a Law School —
"Know Thyself"

There are 201 ABA-approved law schools in the United States. Two hundred are public or private institutions throughout the fifty states, and two of those have only "provisional" accreditation. The 201st accredited school is run by the U.S. Army Judge Advocate General.

While it is important to learn about various law schools while you are an undergraduate, your most important task is to learn about yourself. In general, why do *you* want to go to law school? Do you love to read? Do you like to parse out details? Can you work your way through hundreds, thousands, even tens of thousands of pages of documents on paper, on CDs, on computer files? If not, are you aware this is what lawyers do each day?

Did you take at least one undergraduate course where you read and briefed legal opinions for each and every class (e.g., constitutional law in political science, contract law in business, criminal law in criminal justice, First Amendment law in communication, environmental law in science)? Did you enjoy briefing cases? If not, are you aware this is what law school students do every day for three years?

Why are you considering applying to a particular law school? Where in the country do you want to practice? Do you perform better in larger or smaller classes? How competitive are you? Do you need the hustle and bustle of a big city to feel comfortable? Or will you concentrate and perform better in a more rural setting?

5.1. WHAT NOT TO DO

The most important thing in knowing yourself is knowing "why" you want to go to law school. This is where all your shadowing, mentoring, and research-ing during freshman, sophomore, and junior year pays off. There is no one right answer for why an undergraduate wants to go to law school. It is fine to go to law school with the intent of never practicing law, wanting instead to use the insights and discipline of your legal education as a business man/woman or as an entrepreneur. It is perfectly fine to go to law school because you see it as a challenging and rewarding career that you can be passionate about throughout your life. It is equally fine to go to law school because you like to solve puzzles and resolve conflicts. It is also fine to go to law school because you are committed to public service and see law as the right avenue to service.

Do not go to law school simply because it is what your parents or family expects of you. Do not go to law school because you do not know what else to do after graduation.

Once you know "why" you want to attend law school, your next task is to discover the law school where you will thrive and excel. Here are some very simple rules. Do not break any of them.

- Don't choose a particular law school because your father, mother, uncle, aunt, brother, or best friend attended that school!
- Don't measure the quality of any law school based solely on the *U.S. News and World Report* rankings!
- Don't choose a particular law school solely because you think right now that you will be practicing a particular brand of law (IP, environmental, computer, elder, etc.)!
- Don't choose to go to law school because of any movie, TV program, or book! And above all else:
- Don't choose to go to law school by default!

5.2. AREAS OF EMPHASIS

Many college and university undergraduates think about law schools as they do about undergraduate schools, assuming there are multiple departments and programs to major in; but nothing could be further from the truth. These students read up on law schools and believe they need to attend one of five specific law schools if they want to practice "computer law," or a different set of three law schools to have entry into "international law," or one of four still different schools to practice "immigration law."

Stop. What is important is that you find a law school where you will excel.

If you finish in the bottom 20 percent of your law school class, do you think it will matter whether you took the most sophisticated "computer law" class on the West Coast or were taught by the best "international law" professor on the East Coast?

Law schools do not produce specialists; they produce generalists. The entire law school curriculum is designed to produce generalists. The first year of law school is heavily, in some places entirely, composed of common law courses (contracts, torts, property, civil procedure) along with criminal procedure, criminal law, constitutional law, and legal writing.

The second year of law school is generally composed of "code" courses and courses needed for the bar examination. Second-year code courses can include personal tax, corporate tax, the Uniform Commercial Code, and bankruptcy. Second-year bar courses can include evidence, corporations, trust and estates, conflict of laws, federal courts, and professional responsibility (e.g., another code "The ABA Model Rules of Professional Conduct"). Many students also take trial advocacy and/or appellate advocacy. Occasionally, second-year law students can enroll in a clinical course (taxation, housing, criminal prosecution, etc.) but often those courses are reserved for third-year law students.

In third year, you may be able to take one or two elective courses in an area of law that particularly interests you, like "international law," "environmental law," or "immigration law." But there is still a great deal to learn about "labor law," "administrative law," "estate planning," "products liability," or "family law."

The fact is that even top-tier law schools may offer no more than one or two courses in international law, and those will not be offered every semester or even every year. I took only one course in environmental law during my time in law school but spent twenty-two years practicing it. During law school, you do not want to specialize in anything, you want to acquire the analytical, investigative, communication, and rhetorical skills that will serve you in any area of the law.

5.3. LAW SCHOOL RANKINGS

The deans of many law schools will tell you not to look at or pay attention to the law school rankings that appear each year in *U.S. News and World Report* or *Princeton Review* as well as on multiple websites. Do you really need *U.S. News* to inform you that Yale, Harvard, Berkeley, Stanford, Columbia, Chicago, Virginia, Northwestern, Penn, NYU, Michigan, Duke, Cornell, and Georgetown jockey for position in the top fifteen almost every year? For those rare undergraduates bound and determined to score 177 or 178 on the LSAT and to obtain a Supreme Court clerkship, it probably does matter whether you went to Harvard or Yale as opposed to Penn and Duke.

But for the rest of the world, does it really make sense to be obsessing about rankings in *U.S. News*? If you were fortunate enough to be accepted at both George Washington, ranked twentieth, and Notre Dame, ranked twenty-second, do you automatically choose GW as the higher ranked school? Aren't the facts that GW is located in the nation's capital and admits approximately 490 first-year law students, while Notre Dame is located in a small Midwestern town, South Bend, about an hour outside of Chicago, and admits approximately 170 first-year law students equally or more important in your consideration of how you may fit at the schools than two points in the rankings?

Or, suppose you were fortunate enough to be admitted to Ohio State, George Mason, Maryland, Colorado, and Wake Forest? Can you choose based on rankings? The first three are all tied at thirty-ninth and the last two are tied at forty-fourth.

Do you want a public law school or a private law school? Do you want an urban school with multiple "clinical" options perhaps in a state capital? Or, do you want a more pastoral setting with fewer distractions? Do you qualify for lower in-state tuition at one of them? Which school is closest to the area of the country where you would like to end up practicing law? Have you visited each school while it was in session? Where did you feel most comfortable and at home? All of these questions are more important than who is ranked highest.

Do you even know the "factors" that go into the algorithm that churns out the numerical rankings in *U.S. News*? Unfortunately, what has become tragically apparent over the past few years is that law school administrators at both public and private law schools manipulated the "data" their school was submitting each year to the ABA to gain points in the "rankings." Among the data being manipulated by law school administrators were GPAs and LSAT scores to make the student body at their law school appear to be getting better and better each year.

A major Midwestern public law school admitted to "adjusting" the data for as much as seven years. In the aftermath of the Great Recession of 2008, other law schools actually hired their own graduates in low-paying, short-term, part-time positions to artificially inflate their employment rates for their graduates. The ABA found many schools using devices like this to claim employment for 10 percent and more of their graduates. Angry unemployed law school graduates, who have no way to pay back their loans, filed lawsuits for misrepresentation against a handful of law schools. As many as twenty additional lawsuits are currently threatened.

This does not mean that the rankings can be totally ignored. It does matter if a law school makes it into the top tier of fifteen to twenty-five. Knowing the school you plan to attend is in the top fifty or sixty of the two hundred and one ABA-accredited law schools in the United States can be reassuring. You should be able to feel the law school you selected possesses a solid reputation, a good alumni network, and that you can reasonably compete for your first legal job.

If a law school is at the very bottom of the rankings, you need to ask yourself: what are the chances of good employment if I finish in the middle or lower part of the class? Will the financial cost of three years' lost employment, plus tuition, fees, and expenses ever be recoverable? As seen in the next chapter, the "How Do I Pay for It?" question is a very serious question.

5.4. WEBSITES TO KNOW

When choosing the law schools to which you will apply, there are four absolutely critical websites where you need to become a constant visitor. The first is *LSAC.org*. The second is *The ABA-LSAC Official Guide to ABA-Approved Law Schools*. The third is the *Boston College Law School Locator*. And the fourth is the *ABA Section on Legal Education and Admissions to the Bar*.

The LSAC website is your starting point for all things law school related. This includes how to open and use an LSAC account, the dates for future LSATs, data from past tests, including data on students who take the test a second time, information on legal careers, details on the law school application process, LSAC's Credential Assembly Service, and much more.

The ABA-LSAC Official Guide is published each year in hard copy and can be found in your pre-law advisor's or career service advisor's office. It is also available conveniently online for free. By clicking on any of the fifty states or the District of Columbia, you will immediately jump to a page that identifies every accredited law school in that jurisdiction, its location, and the cost to submit an application. By clicking on the law school's name, you immediately jump to a screen which allows you to access two pages of "data" on the specific law school as well as two pages of "description" prepared by the law school about its unique programs. Among the critical data to be found for each and every school are tuition and other costs, number of applicants, number of first year students, their ethnic composition, their twenty-fifth percentile and seventy-fifth percentile GPA scores, and their twenty-fifth percentile and seventy-fifth percentile LSAT scores. The *Official Guide* is affectionately referred to by pre-law students as the Bible.

The *Boston College Law School Locator* is updated each year and essentially repackages the ABA-LSAC data into an even more user-friendly form. Utilizing a block or chart format, the *Locator* places GPAs on the vertical axis going from less than 2.6 to greater than 3.6 in seven blocks. The *Locator* then places LSAT scores on the horizontal axis from a low of less than 145 to a high of greater than 165 in six blocks. You can "locate" where your personal GPA and personal LSAT score fall and, going to that juncture, click on the box to see law schools where your credentials might be competitive. Naturally, Box A with GPAs above 3.6 and LSATs above 165 includes Yale, Harvard, Stanford, Duke, and Columbia. Box S, the lowest box, with a GPA of greater than 2.8 and an LSAT score of greater than 145 includes Nova Southeastern, Detroit Mercy, Faulkner, Ohio Northern, and Florida Coastal, among others. The same twenty-fifth percentile and seventy-fifth percentile GPAs and LSAT scores from the *Official Guide* are also listed for each school. In addition, the *Locator* provides a link to each of the individual law schools' websites. By clicking on any school's name, whether it is Yale or Nova Southeastern, you are immediately taken to the law school's home page and can investigate and read about each law school as much as you like.

5.5. ALL THE SAME BUT DIFFERENT

Most law schools are very similar to one another. Not only are the first-year classes often identical, they often use identical text books. As you read up on the faculty at different law schools, even they will begin to appear "fungible"—law school speak for interchangeable. Whether you are attending the twenty-fifth- or the fiftieth- or the seventy-fifth-ranked law school, most of the faculty who will teach your first-year common law courses all come from the top tier of fifteen to twenty law schools and by and large all received the same training. The amount and degree of difficulty of the course work is also fairly consistent.

The "code" courses discussed earlier are also unavoidably similar. The federal rules of evidence or the rules of civil procedure, the bankruptcy code or tax code, and the Uniform Commercial Code don't change from law school to law school.

And today, essentially every law school offers its own law review and its own version of trial advocacy, moot court, and negotiation, along with a variety of clinical programs. The clinical programs allow law school students to experience hands-on work in areas from child advocacy, to tax preparation, to housing and landlord-tenant disputes, to semester-long placements with defenders, prosecutors, and courts.

Despite all the similarities, there are important differences between law schools, not including the *U.S. News* rankings discussed previously. Some of these differences are embedded and will not change from year to year. They arise from the location of the school and the size of the first-year class. Indiana, Fordham, and Iowa are all ranked next to each other. But Bloomington, New York City, and Iowa City are all very different places. And first-year class sizes of 230, 410, and 180 can also create different atmospheres. This recognition returns us to our earlier issue that you must "know yourself."

How well do you work in a big metropolis? Have you always been in a smaller college or university with class sizes of thirty or forty, or have you attended a large public university with two hundred plus students in a classroom? How will either background impact your ability to excel in law school?

In addition, there are societal differences among law schools that appear to arise from the specific mix of administrators, faculty, and students over any given five-year period. These differences do seem to vary over time and these differences may be critical to your success at the school you choose. Are the law students competitive or cooperative, fighting for every grade, or willing to help out a classmate? Do administration or faculty encourage and reward competition? How well do you handle competition? Is there a friendly feeling when you walk through the school or shadow a student for a day? Or is everyone stressed and on edge? How well do you handle stress? What sorts of diversity characterize a school—gender, ethnicity, race, geography? How do you handle diversity or the lack of diversity at a school? These societal differences can sometimes be glimpsed on law school websites but are most often picked up during campus visits by watching the interaction of faculty with students and students with one another. I encourage my students to arrange a day visit at every law school where they are admitted prior to making their first payment to hold a seat in the 1L class.

5.6. CAREERS CAN CHANGE

No one can tell you with certainty what will be the next "hot" or "up-and-coming" area of law when you graduate from law school. During my twenty-two years of practice, large and midsized firms saw periods during which real estate law and corporate mergers and acquisitions flourished, followed by a quite different period when bankruptcy, intellectual property, or white-collar crime flourished.

I am not even sure anyone can, with confidence, name all, or any, of the potential areas of law that may flourish over the next decade. Will it be elder law for an aging population; transnational law for the global economy; or some new variant of business law, tax law, or IP law for the hundreds and thousands of small businesses springing up online each day?

What I can assure you is that your legal career, if it lasts long enough, will go through many stages in which you must reinvent and retool yourself, relying on the communication skills and logical reasoning ability you developed in law school and in practice.

My first mentor began his career as an in-house attorney for a large steel company, became for many years a litigation partner at a major national firm, and is completing his career as a solo practitioner. As a litigator, he began handling labor cases for a railroad, worked for a while in products liability, and then spent a great deal of time in environmental law. Obviously, he successfully reinvented his legal career a number of times.

It is important to understand that if you join a law firm as an associate, your area of practice will not always be of your choosing. Your practice area could easily be where the firm needs you most when you are hired. In my earliest years with the law firm, I was lucky to be able to handle some First Amendment cases, but I also was a bottom-tier associate on large construction law cases where all I did was review documents and summarize depositions. Later, I was able to do a little bit of international law involving intricate parts of the Geneva Convention, as well as two fascinating intellectual property cases, one about apple juice and the other about computer chips. But throughout all twenty-two years, I did environmental law. During my three years of law school, I took no construction law, no international law, and no intellectual property law whatsoever. I did take one First Amendment course and one environmental law course.

It may sound trite when you read in every book you pick up that law schools train you "to think like a lawyer," but it is the truth. It is not the substance of particular courses in law school that will make or break your career, rather it is how well you learned to think, to analyze, to work, to reason, and to dissect as a lawyer.

Chapter Six

How Do I Pay for It?

It is never too early for undergraduates and their parents to begin the discussion of "how do I pay for law school?" In the spring of 2012, an article appeared in the journal *PLANC POINTS*: *Newsletter of the Pre-Law Advisors National Council* titled "Preparing Students for the Financial Realities of Legal Education." The author, Heather Jarvis, noted that she graduated from Duke University School of Law over a decade ago with $125,000 in debt.

So what is the reality? Ms. Jarvis points out that law school tuition rose approximately 320 percent from 1989 to 2009 and is continuing to rise each year. Her article suggests that "public" law school tuition averaged $18,471 in 2009 while "private" law school tuition averaged $35,743. But tuition is not the sole cost of law school. With the "other" costs (books, room, board, commuting, health insurance, etc.) averaging between $12,500 and $25,000 depending on where in the United States the law school is located, total average legal educational costs ranged from a low of $30,971 to a high of $60,743 per year. Thus, Ms. Jarvis estimates three years of law school education costs a student between $93,000 and $183,000. How will you pay for this?

6.1. DON'T COUNT ON SCHOLARSHIPS

Historically, law schools, unlike undergraduate programs, provide very little in the way of scholarship money. Moreover, even when some scholarship money is available, the money is not always committed for the full three years. You need to read the fine print on the duration and conditions of law school scholarships very carefully. Law schools tend to use their limited scholarship money to attract top credentialed candidates. But some scholarships are only "guaranteed" for the first year (1L), and after that students are offered loan programs. Also since scholarships are meant to attract and retain top candidates, some law schools "redistribute" their scholarship funds at the end of first and second year so that the money always goes to the top performers. As set forth in the following, most students fund their law school education by way of public and private loans that must be repaid. The article by Heather Jarvis, discussed previously, suggests that by 2009 the "typical" public law school graduate borrowed $68,827 and the typical private law school graduate borrowed $106,249 to finance their legal education.

6.2. TUITION, BOOKS, LIVING EXPENSES EQUALS?

The ABA-LSAC Official Guide to ABA-Approved Law Schools is the key source to get a handle on actual current law school educational costs. Every ABA-approved law school must submit its "data" each year and that data includes "tuition" and "living" costs. The combined total is that school's estimate of your law school educational cost for one year. These costs will vary depending upon the reputation of the law school, the area of the country, and whether the school is public (state supported) or private.

For public law schools, two tuition figures will be listed: one for residents (R) and one for nonresidents (NR). Below are the costs for law schools in five states across the country (Massachusetts, South Carolina, Illinois, Colorado, and Oregon) for the 1L class which started in August of 2011. The data comes from the *ABA-LSAC Guide*. I start with Massachusetts because the northeastern corridor contains some of the most sought after and most highly priced law schools.

Massachusetts is home to seven ABA-approved law schools; all are private law schools with yearly total education costs between $57,013 and $70,100.

Law School	Tuition	Living	Year	Three Years
Boston College	$40,905	$18,690	$59,595	$178,785
Boston Univ.	$40,838	$17,618	$58,456	$175,368
Harvard	$46,616	$23,484	$70,100	$210,300
New Eng. Boston	$39,990	$17,780	$57,779	$173,310
Northeastern	$41,066	$19,500	$60,566	$161,689
Suffolk	$41,120	$22,113	$63,243	$189,729
W. New England	$36,854	$20,159	$57,013	$171,039

South Carolina, on the other hand, is home to only two ABA-approved law schools, one public and one private.

Law School	Tuition	Living	Year	Three Years
Charlestown	$35,606	$19,250	$54,958	$164,568
Univ. S. Carolina	$20,236 (R)	$16,517	$36,753	$110,259
	$40,494 (NR)	$16,517	$57,011	$171,033

At the center of the country, the state of *Illinois* is home to nine ABA-approved law schools, three of which are public and six of which are private.

Law School	Tuition	Living	Year	Three Years
Chicago	$46,185	$21,060	$67,245	$201,735
Chicago–Kent	$40,500	$22,044	$62,544	$187,632
DePaul	$39,350	$23,045	$62,395	$187,185
Illinois	$36,420 (R)	$16,068	$52,488	$157,464
	$43,420 (NR)	$16,068	$59,488	$178,464
John Marshall	$36,920	$26,440	$63,360	$190,080
Loyola	$38,068	$19,900	$57,968	$173,904
Northern Illinois	$17,269 (R)	$15,972	$33,241	$99,723
	$30,960 (NR)	$15,972	$46,932	$140,796
Northwestern	$49,714	$22,048	$71,762	$215,286
Southern Illinois	$14,746 (R)	$14,546	$29.292	$87,876
	$33,097 (NR)	$14,546	$47,643	$142,929

In the west, *Colorado* is home to only two law schools, one private and one public.

Law School	Tuition	Living	Year	Three Years
Univ. of Colorado	$29,915 (R)	$14,919	$44,834	$134,502
	$35,773 (NR)	$14,919	$50,692	$152,076
Denver	$37,152	$16,707	$53,859	$161,577

Finally, in the far northwest, *Oregon* is home to three law schools, two private and one public.

Law School	Tuition	Living	Year	Three Years
Lewis & Clark	$35,095	$18,150	$53,248	$159,744
Univ. of Oregon	$24,032 (R)	$14,460	$38,491	$115,473
	$29,953 (NR)	$14,460	$44,413	$133,239
Willamette	$31,130	$16,740	$47,870	$143,610

Based upon the differences between resident and nonresident tuition at public or state law schools, it is important for students planning on attending a public law school outside of their home state to determine how quickly they can establish resident status and be eligible for the lower resident tuition.

6.3. LIKE BUYING YOUR FIRST HOUSE

The cost of three years of law school education at the twenty-three schools previously discussed ranges from a low of $87,000 at Southern Illinois (if you are a resident) to a high of $215,000 at Northwestern. This is consistent with Jarvis's estimate of $93,000 and $183,000. Public law schools may cause you to incur less debt than private law schools if you are able to get "resident" status. Attending law school in more rural, less urban areas may reduce your debt but may also reduce employment opportunities following graduation. Whatever the actual costs of three years at your chosen law school, this will be the biggest investment a young college or university graduate makes, prior to buying a home or deciding to have a first child with the escalating costs of education.

Thinking of attending law school as buying a home is a useful metaphor. In each case, you need to carefully consider and plan out exactly how you will pay off the mortgage on the home or, in this instance, the law school student loans. However, where the interest rates on home mortgages fell to all-time lows following the 2008 economic collapse, the interest rates on law school student loans remain at staggering levels.

6.4. INTEREST RATES ON LOANS

The *Federal Direct Stafford Loan* remains one of the most common methods of funding law school. The annual Stafford loan limit for law school students is $20,500 per academic year and is available to all students. A FAFSA must be submitted. Interest on the Stafford loan is fixed at 6.8 percent annually and a 1 percent loan fee is deducted. Historically, the Stafford loan was "subsidized" by the federal government, so that the government paid the interest while you were in law school and for the six-month grace period after graduation. But, beginning on July 1, 2012, law school students are no longer eligible to receive "subsidized" Stafford loans. Students will be required to pay the interest accrued on the loan during the three years of law school but can defer payment until after graduation. This obviously increases the size and overall cost of the loan.

The *Federal Perkins Loans* may be available to some students in some law schools. Unlike the Stafford loans, the Perkins loans are based entirely on financial need. A FAFSA must be filed. The interest rate is a bit lower at 5 percent, but the amount which can be borrowed each year is also lower at $8,000.

Graduate PLUS Loans for Law Students may be available to students with a good credit history. PLUS loans are federally guaranteed but carry a high fixed interest rate of 7.9 percent. Beginning on July 1, 2012, a 4 percent loan fee is deducted at disbursement. A FAFSA must be filed.

The Federal Direct Stafford Loan, the Federal Perkins Loan, and the Graduate PLUS Loan may all be eligible to be repaid under the Income-Based Repayment Program (IBR) and/or eligible for inclusion in the Federal Public Service Loan Forgiveness Program (PSLF).

Finally, many *Private Loans* are available to law students with good credit.

Some private lenders offer specific post-graduate loan programs available to study for the bar exam. Interest rates will vary widely. Moreover, many of these loans often require cosigners. Since these private loans are not eligible for inclusion in either IBR or PSLF programs, repayment under current economic conditions can be problematic.

Despite the growing concern about the nation's law schools being able to place all of their graduates in legal jobs, admissions officers at the ABA-approved law schools seem able to find most law school students all of the loans they need to pay the law school tuition and associated costs. In 2009 a graduate of my home institution, who aspired to become a public interest lawyer and return to the same tough streets in North Jersey where she grew up, was unable to obtain admission to the New York City law schools that were her first choices. But she did get accepted at one of the Massachusetts law schools. The school had absolutely no trouble finding her $55,000 in loans per year, $165,000 in debt at graduation, on top of her already existing undergraduate loans.

6.5. YOUR DEBT LIMITS HOW AND WHERE YOU CAN PRACTICE

Legal salaries vary widely based upon where in the country a lawyer is practicing and who the employer is. At the very high end, there continues to be high-paying, big-firm starting salaries in the major metropolitan centers with salaries starting around $155,000 per year. But these positions are only being garnered by the top 10 percent of law school graduates, who are generally coming out as law review editors and/or with federal or state court clerkships.

A *New York Times* article in 2012 shows that the data on starting salaries for attorneys tends to be bimodal with a maximum of 14 percent grouped in the $125,000 to $160,000 range and with over 50 percent grouped in the $35,000 to $55,000 range, and some even lower. In addition, the market for newly minted lawyers took a serious hit with the Great Recession of 2008. The big firms with the highest salaries cut back on hiring and a number even released associates already employed by the firm. Many lawyers graduating law school in 2009, 2010, and 2011 found it a difficult time, for some an impossible time, to land that first full-time legal job.

With ongoing budget concerns at both the federal and state levels, it seems unlikely that the salaries for lawyers in the government or public interest sectors will be rising rapidly. Median starting salaries for government lawyers when they are available is about $52,000. Public interest legal positions, Community Legal Services, Legal Aid, and so forth, are lower still in the $43,000 to $45,000 range. How does a newly graduated lawyer with a lifetime of interest in public service pay off $165,000 in loans with interest rates at 6.8 percent or 7.9 percent on a $44,000 salary? Early planning by undergraduates regarding how they will repay their law school student loans is absolutely critical.

Chapter Seven

The Law School Application Process

This chapter repeats some of the information presented earlier about the junior year. But it is worth repeating. As noted earlier, the application process hinges on the LSAT and when you take the exam; ideally take the LSAT exam in June after your junior year. BUT DO NOT take the exam until you put in the 250 to 300 hours of intensive study required and are certain you are ready to do your best. You cannot know where your credentials (especially your GPA and LSAT score) will be "competitive" and, therefore, cannot realistically be considering where to apply without your LSAT score.

Almost all law school applications are online and can be found on each individual law school's website. While many of the application forms are similar, they generally are not identical. You need to be careful with the wording of each question and with the specific instructions on each application. Your target is to have all of your law school applications completed and submitted before you go home for Thanksgiving in senior year.

During your junior year, you should look at a variety of online applications on various law school websites. Since essay questions on applications can change from year to year, what you are looking at may not be the exact application you will fill out senior year. The actual application you need to fill out will not "go live" (i.e., be available to prospective applicants) until roughly the last week of August at the beginning of senior year. Nonetheless, it is a good idea to review a few application forms during junior year just to gain a sense of the detailed information required on the applications.

7.1. LSAC ACCOUNT

To register to take the Law School Admission Test (LSAT), a student needs to go to Law School Admission Council (LSAC) and select a specific test date, a specific testing center location, and pay the basic registration fee, which in 2012 was $160. There are additional fees for late registration, test date changes, hand scoring, and the like. This is the time to open your personal LSAC account and pay the basic fee of $155 for the Credential Assembly Service (CAS). Each candidate receives his/her own LSAC account number and each account is linked to a specific bar code.

LSAC serves as the clearinghouse which assembles all the materials you need to ultimately send to law schools—your LSAT score, your personal statement, your college or university transcripts, and your letters of recommendation. The transcripts, letters, and statement all are sent in with your personal bar-coded cover sheet and entered into your account, which you can monitor online. When you are ready to submit your application, you simply instruct LSAC to submit your credentials to a particular law school and the entire package goes at one time.

Your LSAC account is good for three years and essentially all of the ABA-approved law schools in the United States utilize the Credential Assembly Service run through LSAC. Note, there are LSAC fee waiver procedures for those who quality, which are explained on their website.

7.2. LSAT SCORE

As discussed previously, the LSAT is a four to five hour, nationally standardized test administered four times each year in June, October, December, and February. For students planning on attending law school immediately following graduation, I encourage them to take the LSAT in June after junior year.

Ideally, I would like to see all law school applications completed and all credentials assembled and sent by Thanksgiving of senior year. To do this, a June test is best. BUT, and this is an important *but*, do not take the test until you are confident you are ready to do your best.

As discussed previously, your LSAT score is the key credential. To attend a solid school, you must get a score of 155 and above; to attend a law school ranked in the top seventy-five you probably need a score of 160. To even break into the top thirty you generally need a score in excess of 165. Both you and LSAC will receive your LSAT score approximately twenty-one days after administration of the test. If the score is not to your liking, there is nothing you can do about it, since it is then "on the books" at LSAC.

You will have opportunities to "cancel" your score after taking the exam but not after the score is sent to you. You may cancel at the conclusion of the test, before you ever turn it in. Or you can cancel within a few days of taking the test. The LSAC website provides you with the details.

In my experience, there are a number of ways to compensate for a poor freshman year in college, but there is next to no way to compensate for a bad performance on the LSAT. Notice that the *Boston College Law School Locator* identifies only five law schools where an LSAT score of 145 or lower even falls into their range and only another twenty-five law schools where a 149 or lower falls into their range. Think of this another way: only 15 percent of the ABA-approved law schools in the entire United States appear willing to accept any candidates with an LSAT score below 150.

7.3. UNDERGRADUATE TRANSCRIPT(S)

The second key credential is your undergraduate GPA. If you plan on having all your law school applications submitted by Thanksgiving as I suggest, your transcript will only cover your first three years. You will need the registrar's office at each institution of higher education you attended to send an "official" transcript with the LSAC bar-coded cover sheet to the Credential Assembly Service. But, beware, your GPA may not be calculated as high as it appears on your current transcript by LSAC.

Many students enroll in summer courses or courses at a community college before they transfer to a private or state university for their final two years. Often the university where you will be graduating transfers in the credits from summer school or community college but not the grades, so only the grades at your current institution are calculated on your official transcript as your GPA. But LSAC goes back and recalculates your "complete" GPA.

A difficult freshman year at a community college where you collected a large handful of C- grades might not impact your GPA on your official transcript but will be counted in by LSAC. The math or science course you took one summer at another institution where all you cared about was getting a C to allow the credits to transfer back to your home institution can now come back to pull down your GPA. Finally, some colleges and universities allow (sometimes even encourage) students to retake courses where they underperformed with Ds or Fs. Those institutions often include only the second or higher grade when a student retakes the course a second time. But LSAC will count both grades, the original F and the B when the course is retaken, again lowering the anticipated GPA.

Also remember, if your first semester senior year grades improve your GPA, do send the new "official" transcript to LSAC and request that it be sent to all the law schools where you applied.

7.4. PERSONAL STATEMENT

Your law school application will require a personal statement. A personal statement of two to two and one-half pages, double-spaced, twelve-point font is about right. If a law school has five thousand applicants, they do not want to read your senior thesis. Above all, make it "personal"! Many undergraduate students find it extremely difficult to write about themselves. July and August before senior year, after you have taken the LSAT, is a good time for self-reflection and planning your personal statement. What experience made you the man or woman you now are, as you look toward law school? Was it some hurdle you overcame in school, in life, in sports? Was it a person whose life you touched or who touched your life? Was it a book, a play, a piece of music that inspired and drove you? Was it a loss you suffered through and overcame?

The letters of recommendation, discussed next, are an opportunity for your professors to advocate on your behalf. You are applying to a profession that is all about "advocacy," and the personal statement presents your one big chance to make your voice heard and to advocate for yourself. Think of the personal statement as a trial, with an opening statement, presentation of evidence, and a closing argument. In the first three sentences, you must "hook" the reader in the law school admissions office, and with the evidence presented and final three sentences you must convince the reader that he/she wants you, with your unique personality and skill set, in their first-year law school class.

This is not the time for purple ink, rhetorical flourishes, or cute efforts like writing as if you are a future Supreme Court Justice. This statement is not about who you hope to become, or what you hope to accomplish for the world. This statement is about you right here and right now. How you became who you are and why a law school wants you in its class.

As with the application itself and the resume, your personal statement must be letter-perfect. No errors in grammar, punctuation, diction, or capitalization; no misspelled words, half sentences, or run-on sentences are allowed. Proofreading, as discussed elsewhere, is critical. But the ultimate key is keeping it "personal."

7.5. LETTERS OF RECOMMENDATION

With letters of recommendation there are three basic questions: How many letters of recommendation do you need? Who should write them? What should they say?

Depending upon the law school, you will need two or three letters of recommendation. Each law school's application form will tell you in the "instructions" how many letters of recommendation they want to see. Always obey those instructions.

Generally, your letters of recommendation should be written by college or university faculty who actually observed and evaluated your performance in class. While there are a few minor exceptions, letters from politicians, lawyers, or distinguished alumni of the law school who often do not know you personally and cannot speak to your specific skill set are not helpful, and can be potentially harmful.

Finally, the letters of recommendation need to provide positive and detailed advocacy, which can often make the difference between acceptance and rejection. The ABA and LSAC both confirm that most law schools are looking for a specific set of skills that will lead to success in law school.

> These include **analytical and problem-solving skills**, **critical reading** abilities, **writing** skills, **oral communication** and listening abilities, general **research** skills, task **organization and management** skills, and the values of serving faithfully the interests of others while also promoting justice. (emphasis added)

Most law school applicants will find the faculty members writing letters of recommendation for them went to graduate school in their particular discipline—English, history, communication—not to law school. If you read diligently about law school and the legal profession during your freshman and sophomore years, as I advise, you will know a good bit more about law school than your professor does.

Therefore, you will need to inform your letter writers that law school admissions officers are looking for specific and detailed facts demonstrating that a student possesses the skills to excel at their law school. For law school letters of recommendation, facts are the highest form of advocacy. *Identifying the specific paper, oral presentation, or exam* where the student excelled will set him/her apart from the thousands of other applicants. *Identifying the research project* where the student's insight, creativity, and analytical skills amazed and delighted the professor will make the letter memorable.

In addition, students also need to help their faculty members remember those events. Beginning with first semester freshman year, you need to "save" and "preserve" your best work. Students tend to remember faculty members much better than faculty remember students; that is simply the reality, given class size at most colleges and universities. An undergraduate student generally has five faculty members per semester. A faculty member at a state university may have 250 to 500 students per semester and even at a small liberal arts college may have 125 students per semester and more.

When you get back a midterm with the grade A+, save it. When you get back a final exam that exclaims "highest grade in the section!"—preserve it. When you submit a PowerPoint presentation that gets an A, keep it. When you get back a research paper with glowing comments on it, save it.

7.6. RESUMES

I encourage students to build a one-page resume with five basic headings (1) Personal Information, (2) Education, (3) Honors and Awards, (4) Experience, (5) Activities, Leadership, Service, and perhaps a sixth, (6) Personal Interests.

Under *Personal Information*, include your full name, home address, school address, telephone number, and e-mail. Just make certain your e-mail address is professional and appropriate. Lovestoparty@yahoo.com or studman23@aol.com are neither professional nor appropriate. Sally.smith or John.smith@gmail.com are fine.

Under *Education*, include your college or university, major, minor, and grade point average (GPA). Do not include high school; do include all undergraduate institutions and any graduate institutions with separate GPAs for each. Do not include a subheading with "selected courses," "representative classes," or the like. The law schools receive all of your undergraduate transcripts and will carefully read them line by line.

As discussed earlier, I am not a fan of "dual majors" because I feel they double the number of 100- and 200-level courses on your transcript and reduce the number of 300- and 400-level courses. But, if you are a double major, include it. If your GPA is below 3.2, some students choose not to place it on their resume, reasoning that it is right there on the transcript. And remember, a lower than desirable GPA may need explanation in an addendum, especially if one semester of illness or a rocky start freshman year produced the problem.

Under *Awards and Honors*, include scholarships, fellowships, semesters on Dean's List, graduation awards, invitations to National Honor Societies, publications, and public service awards. Also include athletic awards from all-American to all-state, case competition awards in intercollegiate business school programs, as well as best advocate or best witness awards in mock trial or moot court competitions.

Under *Experience*, include all work experience since graduating from high school beginning with the most current and working backward; this includes full-time, part-time, and summer-time jobs. Provide beginning and end dates for each position, identifying your specific roles using action verbs.

Under *Activities, Leadership, Service*, include all academic or student affairs programs and clubs (e.g., environmental club, baseball team, student newspaper, yearbook, sororities/fraternities, College Republicans, choral, tennis team, chemistry society, or philosophy club). For each entry, specify the years of your involvement and any leadership roles you played. Also include any service, volunteer, or ministry activities both on and off campus. Volunteer work at Habitat for Humanity or Ronald McDonald House, tutoring struggling high school students, and a service trip sponsored by your church, all can be included here.

Under *Personal Interests* or perhaps *Other*, include languages and your level of proficiency, foreign travel, and hobbies or interests that are unique and will set you apart from other applicants. "Love to read" will not set you apart, "Working on a first novel" could. "Sports" will not distinguish you but "squash racquets," "fencing," or "competitive bicycle racing" might.

Make absolutely certain that everything on your resume is true and correct; exaggerations can come back to haunt you. Also make sure everything is letter-perfect. Do not rely on spell check. Do not rely on proofreading on the computer screen. Print it out and proofread in hard copy. Proofreading to guarantee a letter-perfect document is a difficult task. You wrote the resume; you know what you tried to say. Your mind thinks it is there, even when your eye does not see it. Proofread slowly, use a ruler so that you focus only on the specific line you are proofreading. Law firms know how hard proofreading actually is. For contracts, SEC filings, or public offerings, law firms hire professional proofreaders who work in pairs. From hard copy, not from the computer screen, they read to each other out loud every sentence with every bit of punctuation. For your resume, personal statement, and entire application package, have at least one or two other people read it before you submit it.

7.7. EARLY DECISION

Most law school applications will allow candidates to check off a box that states that the candidate wishes to apply for "Early Decision" status. Agreeing to Early Decision status means that if this particular law school accepts you that you guarantee you will enroll at that law school no matter which other law schools subsequently accept you. This is a very big commitment both on the part of the applicant and on the part of the law school. A law school applicant should never check the box to apply for Early Decision at more than one law school; if you do so, it means you "lied" to at least one of those law schools, and no law school will feel that it can accept or trust you.

Personally, I am not a big fan of Early Decision status, in part because I do not think it positively impacts a decision to admit unless you are already in the presumptively admit pile, in which case you would be admitted, and in part because undergraduates are notoriously bad at estimating those law schools where his/her credentials would be competitive.

Over the years, a few of my highest-quality law school candidates argued with me that they believe checking the Early Decision status box on an application to a top twenty law school, Georgetown or Penn for example, where your credentials do not place you in the presumptively admit pile but where you are still in the mix, may help you get onto the "Wait List" discussed at the end of this chapter.

7.8. ADDENDUM DOS AND DON'TS

Law school applications allow students to submit additional information not required on the application by way of addendum. This is not the chance to write a second personal statement about why you think the school should accept you or how long you have thought about going to law school. An addendum, if any, should be short. My rule of thumb is one-third of a page double-spaced at most. Never over one page. And the addendum needs to be specific. What follows are a few examples of addendum "dos" and "don'ts."

Do explain a GPA discrepancy between freshman year and the rest of your career with an addendum. A GPA of 2.1 freshman year coupled with GPAs in sophomore and junior years of 3.75 will produce a cumulative GPA of 3.2, which is OK but not the stellar 3.75 earned the past two years. A brief three- or four-sentence statement explaining a difficult adjustment your first year away from home or the wrong choice of an initial major, coupled with highlighting the demanding courses you have taken during the last two years can lead to a conclusion, which you do not have to state, that the 3.75 is the more accurate portrait of your academic ability.

Don't explain a low LSAT score or argue that your GPA is a better indicator of your ability. Law schools rely upon the LSAT score as their best predictor of first-year success. Your arguments are not going to change their mind. What you accomplish by such an addendum is, in effect, negative, calling more attention to your low LSAT score. And suggesting that you did not prepare well enough for the LSAT exam simply calls your judgment into question.

Do explain any disciplinary disclosures required by the application. If you have an academic, legal, or campus life disciplinary blot on your undergraduate record, disclose it. Use the addendum to very briefly explain it. Don't try to justify it, or understate it, and above all, don't misrepresent it. Don't try to blame someone else. Explain that you apologized, took your punishment, made restitution (if necessary), and learned your lesson. State, if true, that the transgression happened only once, has not happened since, and will never happen again.

Don't explain why you will become a great lawyer or jurist. The addendum is for factual clarification, not self-advocacy. All self-advocacy belongs in your personal statement.

Do explain by way of addendum any significant change (improvement) in your LSAT score. Law schools believe strongly in the nationally standardized LSAT scores. Once a candidate receives a score of 147 for example, law schools anticipate that a second try at the test may result in a slight improvement but generally expect a second test score to be within two or three points of the original score. An improvement of anything like ten points will cause law schools to be very suspicious of the second score and requires an addendum. If you were coming down with the flu on the day of the first test, or had a death in the family the week of the test, you must write an addendum to explain your score increase from 147 to 156. But remember law schools will question why you did not cancel your score if you actually had the flu and can easily confirm or deny your grandmother's death from a simple internet search.

7.9. DISCLOSURES ADVERTENT AND INADVERTENT

Every law school application asks the candidate to disclose criminal arrests and convictions as well as any disciplinary activity (probation, dismissal, suspension, and the like) during your college or university career. For these advertent disclosure questions, candidates need to read the questions very carefully to be certain they understand exactly what is being asked. Different law schools phrase these questions differently. Then answer the questions directly and succinctly. You need not elaborate or attempt to explain your answer at this point. Often you merely check a box "yes" or "no," and this is where the need for an addendum to explain any "yes" answer arises.

First and foremost, with these advertent disclosure questions you must tell the truth. Lying or misrepresenting criminal actions or academic or student affairs disciplinary actions while in college will come back to haunt you. Law schools know that everyone is human and everyone makes mistakes. A single stupid episode of alcohol in a dormitory or a single act of shoplifting in high school will not bar you from law school. But lying about it could make you appear to the law school admissions committee to be unfit for the study of law and later, since lying to the law school admissions office goes to your character as an adult, can make you appear to the bar examiners to be unfit for the practice of law.

Many law school applications now require a "Dean's Certification" that can confirm that a student's undergraduate record is clean of any disciplinary activity. In addition, law school administrators and state bar associations often revisit undergraduate institutions to satisfy themselves that all questions addressing these advertent disclosures are answered truthfully. If you are not sure what blotches may be on your record, go to your academic dean's office and to the appropriate person in the dean of students' office and find out.

In addition, undergraduates make many inadvertent and sometimes ugly disclosures about themselves and their character which they later learn to regret. Social media has many benefits, it also possesses major downsides. Before you think about applying to law school take time to determine whether there are comments, photographs, or postings on your Facebook page or Twitter account that could strike a law school admissions official as "crude," "inappropriate," "compromising," "biased," "unprofessional," or even as evidence of "illegal" behavior. If so, these comments or pictures will likely be seen and considered, negatively, by the law schools to which you are applying. Many law schools, like numerous employers, now hire admissions personnel whose job is to scan and search the web and social media for information on the applicants under review.

I know law school admissions personnel who communicate all day long through e-mail with hundreds of law school applicants and who complain about inappropriate and vulgar e-mail names or addresses. The way you speak, the way you write, and the way you present yourself to the rest of the world on social media all matter.

You may possess a solid GPA and try to make your resume and personal statement depict an organized, dedicated, and hardworking student. But if the photos posted and the writings on the wall of your Facebook page show you organizing and misbehaving at fraternity keg parties every Thursday night, you will disclose a very different person.

Or, ask yourself, would you want your mom or your dad to read that ugly series of barbs, accusations, and comments thrown back and forth between you and your ex for two weeks on your Twitter account? Do you want the law school admissions staff to read it? The reality is technology, and especially social media, dramatically reduce your realm of privacy, and you need to recognize this.

7.10. HOW MANY APPLICATIONS

Application fees continue to climb for each law school application submitted. During 2012 in the Commonwealth of Pennsylvania, for example, the application fees at the ABA-approved law schools ranged from eighty dollars at the University of Pennsylvania to fifty-five dollars at Pittsburgh with sixty to seventy-five dollars being the midrange. Thus, the number of applications you submit is both a financial and a tactical question.

You certainly do not want to waste $1,000 on applications at schools where your credentials (LSAT score and GPA) don't make you competitive. Over the past five years, graduating seniors applying to law school from my home institution submitted on average eight to nine applications each. Some of them applied to twelve or fifteen law schools, while others applied to only four or five.

As a law school candidate, you must be brutally honest with yourself in deciding where to apply to law school. This application process is not about where you would ideally "like" to go to law school; it is rather about where you can be "accepted" to law school. Your mother may have graduated Penn Law School, and you may have dreamed and worked every day of the past eight years to go to Penn. But if your GPA is 3.5 and your LSAT score is 160, the reality is you are not getting admitted.

Your two most important tools in this process of self-assessment are the *ABA-LSAC Official Guide to ABA-Approved Law Schools* and the *Boston College Law School Locator*. Both are discussed previously, are available online, and will provide you with data on all accredited law schools across the United States. Most importantly, they provide data on the credentials of the prior year's first-year class—including seventy-fifth percentile, median, and twenty-fifth percentile LSAT scores and seventy-fifth percentile, median, and twenty-fifth percentile GPAs. The *Boston College Law School Locator* actually groups law schools in boxes utilizing these criteria.

If your LSAT and your GPA are at or above the median scores at a school, you can consider your self "competitive" at that particular school. Competitive is no guarantee of admission. Many competitive candidates may not get in schools they want due to differences in personal statements, undergraduate institutions, letters of recommendation, diversity, and the like. Keep in mind that squeaking into a law school's "range" at the twenty-fifth percentile for both LSAT and GPA really means you are less than competitive at that school.

Most law school applicants divide their applications into three categories—"competitive" schools, "safe" schools, and "reach" schools. Careful analysis and decision making is required during this process. You will need to balance cost, location, reputation, and competitiveness, as well as bar passage rates and employment data, at a minimum.

If you are going to apply to nine schools, make sure at least two or three are "safe schools," in other words, schools where your LSAT score and your GPA are both at or above the seventy-fifth percentile for last year's incoming law school class. Many undergraduates make the mistake of thinking a school is a "safe school" merely because their credentials are competitive. This mistake can often lead to no law school acceptances at all.

Five or six of your applications need to be at a range of schools where you are truly "competitive," or, where your LSAT and GPA are at or above last year's median for the first-year class. Even then, there is no guarantee that you will receive an offer of admission to one of those schools. For example, undergraduates in Philadelphia are fortunate to have a number of solid law schools in the immediate area, many of which have very similar median credentials. For the first-year law school classes which entered in August of 2011, the following were the published median LSAT and GPA credentials:

Law School	Median LSAT	Median GPA
Drexel	LSAT 159	GPA 3.40
Dickinson/Penn State	LSAT 159	GPA 3.60
Rutgers	LSAT 161	GPA 3.40
Temple	LSAT 162	GPA 3.47
Villanova	LSAT 160	GPA 3.33

Assume you are an undergraduate in the Philadelphia area with a 159 or 160 LSAT score and a 3.50 GPA. You may believe, simply following the numbers, that you are competitive at all five area law schools and confidently apply to all five. But it is quite possible for you to be accepted at none of them. Every law school across the country is looking for diversity: racial, gender, ethnic, and geographic diversity. All five schools in the Philadelphia area will have hundreds, perhaps a thousand, applications just as competitive as your GPA and LSAT from the same local area. Your identical credentials may actually have an increased potential for acceptance at an identically ranked law school located in Maine, Tennessee, Iowa, Texas, or Oregon because to those schools you bring geographic diversity.

Finally, one or two of your applications can be to "reach" schools, in other words, schools where you know your credentials are at best minimally competitive. Here you are willing to basically waste the seventy-to-eighty-dollar application fee because it is a school you would love to attend and maybe someone will find your personal statement so interesting they will accept you.

7.11. FIRST, SECOND, AND THIRD TIERS

Many law school candidates get caught up in the law school "rankings" and attempt to place law schools in "tiers." Each year *U.S. News and World Report* attracts attention when it produces its rankings of law schools based upon a formula which considers a variety of factors including faculty, publications, library, prestige, student credentials, employment rates, numbers of law clerks, and the like.

By and large, the top ten through fifteen positions each year go to Yale, Harvard, Stanford, Columbia, Chicago, NYU, Berkeley, Penn, Virginia, Michigan, Duke, Northwestern, Cornell, Georgetown, and the like. Different individuals and guides to law school appear to treat the concepts of Tier 1, Tier 2, Tier 3, and Tier 4 differently. Obviously, Tier 1 is "legalese" code for the top law schools in the country. But some analysts treat Tier 1 as only the top ten or fifteen schools, while others treat it as the top twenty-five schools. Some major private corporations in their hiring advertisements treat Tier 1 as the top 50 law schools (i.e., the top quarter of the 201 accredited law schools).

The further down the *U.S. News* rankings one goes, the less useful the rankings may be. For example, what is the real difference between Notre Dame and Emory, ranked in the mid-twenties, and William & Mary or UC–Davis ranked in the mid-thirties?

The tiers provide a generic guide for law school candidates and not much more. Attending a Tier 2 or Tier 3 law school, Temple, ranked 58, or Albany, ranked 113, for example, you can obtain a fine law school education with a wide array of clinical programs as well as the opportunity for judicial clerkships and major firm practice. Recently, *U.S. News* stopped ranking schools below 150. The final fifty schools are all simply listed alphabetically as "unranked."

Three warnings about the tierings and rankings are appropriate. *First*, even minor change in the weighting of the factors considered by *U.S. News* could produce a substantial change in the rankings. For example, increasing the amount of weight attached to the "cost" of a law school education would move a whole new set of schools into the top twenty-five.

Second, the ranking system produced some very unhealthy competition among law schools administrations. Over the past four years, law schools with previously unblemished reputations were forced to admit they exaggerated the LSAT scores or GPAs of their incoming classes to move up in the rankings, and/or padded the employment statistics for their graduates to keep up their ranking. While this statistical manipulation was first discovered at some Tier 4 schools, whose graduates subsequently brought suit against their former law schools for misrepresentation, the same thing occurred at well-respected state and private law schools with long histories of producing quality graduates.

Third, if you discover that the only law schools where your credentials will be competitive and will provide you with a chance of acceptance are unranked Tier 4 schools, you need to step back and think. Are you confident that a realistic cost-benefit analysis makes attending this particular law school a reasonable decision for you?

Perhaps, you live in and want to practice law in the cities of Pittsburgh, PA; Dayton, OH; or Providence, RI, and you believe you can excel and finish near the top of your law school class at Duquesne, Dayton, or Roger Williams, all unranked in 2012. Then fine. Or, if you want a law degree not to practice law but to work in your family's business, fine again.

But if you are looking for a promising career with a good paying position, will giving up three years of income and paying over $100,000 to $150,000 to finish in the bottom half of an unranked law school which may not be located in the geographic area where you want to practice actually be a solid investment?

7.12. FORGET RANKINGS MOST OF THE TIME

Other than the exceptional law school candidate seeking admission to schools ranked in the top twenty and the borderline law school candidate covered in warning three just mentioned, I generally urge undergraduates thinking about law school to ignore the rankings. Instead, focus on the *Boston College Law School Locator* and find schools where your credentials are "competitive" as described earlier. Get information from and read up extensively on those schools. Then start to ask yourself the following questions.

Which schools have clinical programs that interest you? Find someone who went to that school, and talk with them. Your pre-law advisor may be able to help here. If you're a city person, which schools are in thriving urban areas? Is it important for you to be near a state capital, for voluntary internships, clerkships, or job prospects? Do you thrive on competition or on cooperation? Law school culture may be critically important to you. Where do you want to practice after graduation from law school? Statistics suggest that most law school graduates get their first full-time legal position within 100 to 150 miles of the law school campus. So geography might matter to you.

Your goal throughout this process is to find a law school where you will thrive and can excel. The proper combination of geographic location, class size, law school culture, curriculum, special programs, and cost is the key here, much more than which law school is ranked forty-eighth and which is ranked sixty-fifth. Rankings you can find in two minutes, but the important information will take time and effort to sort through and balance before you decide where to apply. In these deliberations, utilize your parents, any friends or relatives who attended law school (especially recently), and the pre-law advisor at your undergraduate institution.

7.13. THE "WAIT LIST"

Once you make your decision on where to apply, you will complete and submit the various applications to your "safe" schools, "competitive" schools, and "reach" schools around Thanksgiving of senior year. Then begins the waiting period.

The waiting is never easy. Law schools typically begin to review completed application files around December 1. Files often go into one of three piles of candidates—(1) the "presumptively" admit pile based on the LSAT and GPA, (2) the "presumptively" deny pile based again on the LSAT and GPA, and (3) the needs further consideration or the "maybe" pile. A quick response to one of your applications is often not a positive one. Just as you are in competition with other law school candidates for a limited number of 1L seats, so also law school admissions offices around the country are in competition with one another. Each law school is working to build the best profile possible for their first year class—highest GPAs, highest LSATs, greatest geographic and ethnic diversity.

Every pre-law advisor around the country wants every one of his/her law school candidates to gain acceptance. But that is an unrealistic hope. In recent years, a number of candidates who sit for the LSAT reconsider upon receiving their score and do not apply to law school. Of those who do apply to law school, nationally between 60 percent to 65 percent get admitted to at least one school. That warns you that 30 plus percent of law school applicants never receive any offer of admission, not even from their "safe" schools.

Of those admitted, a percentage decide not to matriculate and never attend law school. Perhaps, on thinking through the cost-benefit analysis suggested previously, they decided law school was not a sound financial decision. Perhaps, some of them received acceptance only at "safe" schools they never really wanted to or intended to attend.

Finally, the waiting will end (sort of) and you will be sent a decision letter from all the law schools to which you applied. Some will say "denied," and you cannot let it depress you; hopefully at least one will say "admitted" and congratulate you. But there is a third possibility: more waiting. Most law schools take a small number of candidates who are neither presumptively admit, nor presumptively deny, and offer them a spot on the law school's "Wait List."

Every law school knows that every candidate they accept applied to competitive, safe, and reach schools. But the law school cannot know where their particular school stands on your list when they accept you. So every law school accepts more first year students than they can handle, expecting and knowing that a significant percentage of these accepted candidates will decline admission.

The ultimate "Wait List" decision-making process is prolonged as one candidate declines Cornell because he/she was accepted at Columbia, another student declines Wake Forest because she/he was accepted at Duke, and still another student declines Rutgers to accept a lesser-ranked school offering a scholarship. And so it goes all across the country. This process is best understood as watching a long winding line of dominos where as each one falls another one changes position as well.

On the one hand, admissions officers cannot afford to have too many students confirm their acceptances and matriculate because the school will not have enough space to accommodate them. On the other hand, admissions officers also cannot afford to fall ten students short of a target first-year class of, let us say, 250 because at a private law school that amounts to a financial loss close to $500,000 in just one year or $1,500,000 over the three-year life span of that law school class.

The emergency valve for all these law school admissions officers is the "Wait List" composed of candidates whose credentials were in the "maybe" pile, candidates who are generally "competitive" at the school but perhaps not quite as high ranking or diverse as other initially accepted students. Making the "Wait List" is no guarantee that an acceptance will ever materialize and can be nerve-wracking. Wait-listed students can receive offers of admission throughout June, into July, and even as late as August in some cases. It all depends on where and when all the dominos fall.

One final twist on the "Wait List" is tied to the Early Decision process described earlier. Some high-quality law school candidates with excellent GPAs and LSAT scores in the mid-160s believe that checking the box on the application form asking to be considered for Early Decision at a "reach" school, like Cornell or Georgetown, where their credentials may be just at or slightly below the twenty-fifth percentile (so that they did not receive the presumptively deny letter) may increase the possibility not of being accepted initially but rather of being wait listed. I have no data to suggest whether this "tactic" works or is a complete waste of time. But it makes sense to me that even top-tier law schools want candidates on their "Wait List" who will agree to attend even if not contacted until June or July. Remember you can apply to only one school for Early Decision because by checking that box on the application form you are guaranteeing that if accepted by the school you will come.

Chapter Eight

Acceptance — The Holy Grail

The time period between the last week of November or first week of December when you submitted all your completed applications, with your transcripts, personal statement, other required essays, and letters of recommendation, and when you receive the first "decision" letter drags very slowly for law school candidates. There is nothing you can do now except wait and worry. Will my 157 LSAT be enough? Why didn't I take freshman year classes more seriously? But, it is now out of your hands.

By February, candidates are waiting and watching day by day. But often the first word does not come until March. Sometimes the first words are the dreaded "not admitted." Some candidates tell no one, not their roommate, not their pre-law advisor, and certainly not their parents. But they worry. What if no one accepts me? What then?

8.1. I CAN BREATHE NOW

You can tell when the first "acceptance" is received. When that finally happens, candidates want to tell you their news. As they approach your office, you can see it in their faces and in their gait before they even speak. They are smiling, relaxed, looking as if some great weight was lifted from them. Each year many say the same thing: "I think I can breathe now." It does not matter if that first acceptance arrives from your back up "safe" school or your hoped-for "reach" school. You are in; you are accepted; you accomplished it. The worry "what do I do if no one accepts me?" disappears.

You will still be waiting, all through March and sometimes into April, until you hear one way or another from all the law schools to which you applied. There will still be disappointments and "not admitted" responses. But it is all different once you are "in"; as one student said to me, "it's no longer life threatening."

8.2. VISITING SCHOOLS—STAY THE DAY

Let's assume you are fortunate to be "admitted" to two or three law schools. You have time to decide before you put down a small payment to hold the seat, and a longer time before the first large deposit is due. Hopefully, you were able to speak to a current student or a recent graduate of the law school before you decided to apply. Now is the time to visit each law school which accepted you before you make a final decision on where to put down a nonrefundable deposit.

While most law schools quite rationally do not want thousands of "applicants" attempting to visit during the fall admissions process, once you are "accepted" most law schools will accommodate a request for a visit during the spring semester. I encourage you to find a first- or second-year law student who will let you shadow them for a day. Your undergraduate pre-law advisor may be able to assist you here.

Attend classes with your host, go to lunch with students, read in the library for a while, sit in on a study group, watch the interaction between students as well as the interaction between students and faculty both in the classrooms and in the hallways. If you can, spend the entire day so that you absorb a sense of the culture at that particular law school. Visiting right before second-semester exams when the stress levels are highest is not the best nor is a visit during the summer when the law school largely empties out.

8.3. WHAT IS MY LONG-TERM GOAL?

Visiting the law schools where you are accepted can be a big help in deciding where to attend, but you must also now go back to the self-analysis and balancing that led you to apply to your particular set of law schools in the first place. In the application process, you considered a combination of major factors: geographic location, law school ranking, class size, law school culture, curriculum, special programs, bar passage rates, employment rates, and cost.

Now, when you must finally decide where to attend, one or more of these factors will likely carry greater weight. What is your long-term goal? If your goal and passion is to become a prosecutor, perhaps the law school with the best trial advocacy program as well as clinical programs with the district attorney's office or the U.S. Attorney's Office will make your decision easier. If your goal is to obtain a federal clerkship as entrance into a mega firm practice, perhaps the law school with a recent reputation for placing students in clerkships and where you believe you have the strongest opportunity of making law review will turn out to be the best choice for you. If you are entering law school with a great deal of unpaid undergraduate debt and are extremely concerned about how you will pay for law school loans, perhaps the state law school with the most reasonable tuition is a better choice for you than the private law school with a higher ranking but double the tuition.

Each individual law school candidate must go through this balancing decision on his/her own. You can bounce ideas and options off your family and friends, off your teachers and pre-law advisors, but in the end this decision is about "your" long-term goal, not theirs.

8.4. WHERE CAN I FLOURISH?

This decision is not simply about rational choices and means to ends. You are going to be spending sixty plus hours a week for the next three years in class, in the library, at your apartment reading, studying, and outlining the law. You are going to face struggle, stress, competition, frustration, and perhaps disappointment or failure. Your social life will surely suffer, perhaps even disappear, during first and second year. You will spend parts of those three years overworked, underappreciated, and sleep deprived.

To survive all this, you need to be in an environment where you can thrive despite the pressures, the work, and the lack of sleep. This is why visiting the law schools where you are accepted is so important. Despite the inevitable headaches that come with law school, if you are in a culture that is comfortable for you the results you achieve will be better. More important still, you will be a happier law school student. The goal in law school is first to survive and then to thrive and flourish.

8.5. THE SUMMER BEFORE LAW SCHOOL

Many college and university graduates see the summer before law school as a final opportunity to party, hang out with friends, go to the shore, relax, and generally celebrate their success as an undergraduate and in gaining admission to law school. All that is fine. But while you are enjoying what may be your last summer of freedom, set up a productive reading plan for your summer as well.

Your summer reading plan should contain both legal and nonlegal components; and the nonlegal may be the more important. Recall in the opening chapter I encouraged you to follow your passions and to cultivate and expand them as a lawyer. Your personal interests in art, music, poetry, literature, biography, history, or archeology are what make you a vibrant person and help you in all your personal interactions whether it is meeting new friends or interviewing with law firms.

8.6. PROPOSALS FOR A LEGAL READING PLAN

Start with original source documents: *Magna Carta, Declaration of Independence, Constitution,* some of *The Federalist Papers,* and some of the *Anti-Federalist Papers,* especially Brutus. Then proceed on to core Supreme Court opinions, especially if you did not take a constitutional law course as an undergraduate. Read the entire opinion, not a textbook summary. A good cross-section would be *Marbury v. Madison, McCullough v. Maryland, Gibbons v. Ogden, Youngstown Sheet &Tube Co. v. Sawyer, Brown v. Board of Education, U.S. v. Nixon, Chevron v. NRDC, Celotex Corp. v. Catrett,* and *Lopez v. United States.* All Supreme Court opinions can be obtained and downloaded from Cornell University Law School's Legal Information Institute (LII). You should also listen to some classical and contemporary arguments before the Supreme Court, which were preserved on tape and are now digitized by the *Oyez Project.*

Then read a few very basic common law cases in torts or in contracts to become accustomed to the language and ideas in the English "common law" which occupy such a prominent place in first-year law school. Read *Hadley v. Baxendale, Palsgraff v. Long Island RR Co.,* and *Wood v. Boynton.* Then you should enter the contemporary debate about what it is that judges do when they issue opinions deciding cases—for example, Justice William Rehnquist, "The Notion of a Living Constitution," in the *Texas Law Review*; Justice Antonin Scalia, *Interpretation*; and Justice Stephen Breyer, *Active Liberty.*

Finally, buy, read this summer, and then reread again in law school either Goldstein and Lieberman's *The Lawyers Guide to Writing Well* or Garner's *Legal Writing in Plain English*; I prefer the former.

8.7. PROPOSALS FOR A NONLEGAL READING PLAN

The goal of this list is to keep actively reading and learning in new areas and about new fields. Try history or biography, one of my favorite historians is Joseph Ellis, especially *Founding Brothers, American Sphinx,* or *American Creation,* as well as Walter Isaacson's biographies of Kissinger, Steve Jobs,

Benjamin Franklin, and Einstein. Don't neglect the areas of science and religion, for example, Stephen Hawking's *A Briefer History of Time*, *Standing on the Shoulders of Giants*, and *The Grand Design*; or Francis Collins's *The Language of God: A Scientist Presents Evidence for Belief*; or Krista Tippett's *Einstein's God* and *Speaking of Faith*.

In archeology and anthropology, try anything by Loren Eiseley—*The Star Thrower*, *The Immense Journey*, *The Unexpected Universe*, or *The Man Who Saw Through Time*; as well as Ceram's *Gods, Graves and Scholars*; or Curtis's *The Cave Painters: Probing the Mysteries of the World's First Artists*; or just go the website for the Caves at Lascaux and marvel.

For classical literature try, Aeschylus—*Oedipus Rex*, *Antigone*, and *Oedipus at Colonus*, if you have not read them before; anything by Jane Austen; Ivan Turgenev's *Fathers and Sons*; Melville's *Billy Budd*; and Shakespeare—anything, but especially the political plays if you have not read them—*Coriolanus*, *Othello*, *Merchant of Venice*, *King Lear*, *Julius Caesar*, *Macbeth*; Dickens's *Hard Times*, *Great Expectations*, and *Bleak House*; Joseph Conrad's *Heart of Darkness* and *Lord Jim*; Thoreau's *Walden* and his essays on John Brown; George Orwell's *Collected Essays*; T. S. Elliott's *Collected Poems*, *Murder in the Cathedral*; Hemingway's *The Nick Adams Stories*, *A Farewell to Arms*, *Islands in the Stream*.

In contemporary literature, Gore Vidal's novels *Lincoln*, *Burr*, or *Empire*; Thomas Bolt's *A Man for All Seasons*; Tom Wolfe's *Bonfire of the Vanities*; Thomas Mann's *The Magic Mountain*; or my favorite contemporary—Annie Dillard's *Pilgrim at Tinker Creek*, *For the Time Being*, or *An American Childhood*.

The idea here is to build your own list around your own passions and feed your interests. The summer before law school is an ideal time to remind yourself why you loved learning and loved reading in the first place.

Chapter Nine

The First Year—There Are No Second Chances

In my mind, law school should not be thought of as three years, but rather as "one intensive year." As I attempt to explain in the following, there are no second chances; you cannot squander your first year of law school.

The transition to law school is simply not equivalent to the transition to college. Many students graduating from high school struggle during their first year of college or university. Those struggles can be triggered by a variety of factors: more demanding courses, an increased reading load, greater competition, freedom or the lack of supervision, poor time-management skills, lack of self-discipline, weak organizational skills, over-socializing, or addiction to video games. A mediocre or even horrible freshman year in college does not necessarily end your pursuit of a legal career.

However, a mediocre or bad first year in law school can slam closed many career doors. Law review, rank in class, access to clinical programs, interviews for summer associate positions after second year, even judicial clerkships, all depend in various ways upon your first-year grades. Just as you want to take the LSAT once and only once, doing your very best, so also with your first year in law school (1L) you want to be at your best and to do your very best.

9.1. TRANSITION AND SUCCESS

For the first year of law school, you must hit the ground running. You need your housing settled, your finances straightened out, your transportation to and from class set, textbooks purchased, and at least a draft study schedule prepared two or three weeks before class begins.

The best analogy to why you must hit the ground running is the jump college football players experience going into the National Football League, where rookies discover that everyone in the game is now faster, stronger, harder working and more aggressive than the players in college. Every one of the men and women in your 1L class possess GPAs like yours and LSAT scores like yours. You are now engaged in a new level of competition for A grades (which can be rationed in many law schools), for rank in class, for GPAs, for law review, for summer clerkships, for federal and state court clerkships, and ultimately for full-time jobs.

Two places to go to read about the first year are Scott Turow's autobiographical account of his first year at Harvard Law School called *One L, The Turbulent True Story of a First Year at Harvard Law* and Andrew McClurg's *1L of a Ride: A Well-Traveled Professor's Roadmap to Success the First Year of Law School*. Recall that the Great Recession of 2008 exaggerated all the pressures law school brings by making opening-level legal jobs scarce.

Unlike college, you do not get a great deal of orientation at the start of law school, and you do not get the first few weeks to socialize and learn about your classmates, or where the cafeteria is, or how the library is arranged and where you can study in peace. You also do not get to ease into classes. First class assignments are usually a few hundred pages long and are sent out about two or three weeks prior to the start of class. You are expected to arrive at the first class in each course with the reading and briefing complete and ready to "start running."

9.2. CURRICULUM AND BRIEFING

A fairly standard first-year law school curriculum might include courses in contracts, torts, civil procedure, property, criminal law, constitutional law, and legal writing. Depending upon the law school you attend, some of these courses may be either three or four credits, others may be six credits (spread across two semesters). Generally, first-year students take either four or five courses per semester. Some law schools allow for an elective in the second semester, most do not.

Assume that your law school requires for first semester: Torts, four credits; Contracts, three credits (each semester); Civil Procedure, three credits; Property, three credits (each semester); and Criminal Law, three credits (total sixteen credits); and for second semester requires Property II, three credits; Contracts II, three credits; Constitutional Law, four credits; Legal Research and Writing, three credits; and one three-credit elective (total sixteen credits).

During your first year, each class will use a casebook composed primarily of old English common law cases with difficult language and unfamiliar concepts (detrimental reliance, fee simple, mens rea, mutual mistake of fact, and the like). These textbooks are not like college or university textbooks in history or biology, they contain very little, if any, explanatory or descriptive material, and instead are composed largely of old decided cases in English and American law. For each class each week, you will need to "brief" all cases assigned for that class.

Briefing means (1) identifying the key "facts," (2) locating and understanding the "legal question(s)" posed by the specific facts of the case, (3) knowing the "answer(s)" provided by the court to the legal question(s), and, (4) most importantly, unraveling the court's "legal reasoning" in reaching its decision. At the start of first year, this may include no more than understanding the "black letter law" (i.e., the legal principles articulated by the court, or the fundamental components of a contract, "offer," "acceptance," and "consideration"). Later in the year, you will be developing the skill of seeing how slight modifications in the facts or in the bargaining position of the contracting parties change the ways in which the principles are applied by the courts. This requires seeing and understanding the case from multiple perspectives and articulating the underlying policy choices.

Each course may ask you to brief a number of such cases for each class and 1L students find the effort to stay current is a constantly growing pressure.

9.3. THE READING LOAD

If you do not like to read, you should ask yourself why you want to go to law school or to practice law. Assume each of your five courses assigns you sixty pages per week of reading. That estimate may be low, since it would require only twenty pages per class hour for a three-credit course and only fifteen pages per class hour for a four credit course. That is only a total of three hundred pages per week. Robert Miller's *Law School Confidential*, a text composed of reflections by actual law school students, suggests the following:

> The typical law student will *read in excess of three thousand pages* of case law, hornbooks, and outlines *during a fifteen-week semester.* In that semester of 105 days, that means roughly thirty pages of reading every day if you read seven days a week without ever taking a day off. At an average reading rate of ten pages per hour, that means *three hours of reading per day, every day, with no weekends, holidays, or excuses.* Naturally, that's an unrealistic expectation—but realize, of course, that when you start taking days off, the missed reading starts backlogging and piling up on other days. *In my own experience,* in the first year of law school, *I generally read for about four hours a day, six days a week.* That of course, is in addition to class time, and time spent outlining what you've read. *But we are not talking about the time commitment yet, just the reading.* Recognize what you are signing up for. If you can't

fathom yourself reading law for about four hours a day, six days a week, you
might want to start reevaluating your career choice. *Law School Confidential*,
2003, page 27, (emphasis added)

Since this reading material is dense and often unfamiliar, *Law School Confidential's* suggested reading time may actually be low.

Thus time in class (sixteen hours) and time reading (twenty-one hours)
averages out to almost forty hours a week, a full-time job. Not included in
this calculation is time spent briefing, time spent outlining for the final examination, time spent in study groups, and time spent with hornbooks such as
Prosser on Torts trying to grasp "gross negligence," "attractive nuisance," or
"abnormally dangerous activity."

Law School Confidential's calculation also does not include time spent
sleeping, cooking, eating, performing errands, or traveling to and from
school. It also certainly does not include your personal life which, like your
sleep, will inevitably suffer during your first year.

While one of my messages throughout this *Handbook* is to maintain your
individual passions, which make you a unique and interesting person, especially during the first year of law school there will be precious little time for
nights out dancing, pickup basketball, video games, Facebook, Twitter, or
text messaging. And yes, you will get used to it, if you want to excel.

9.4. SOCRATIC METHOD

The current law school "Socratic method" is Socratic in style only, but not in
substance Platonic. Its goal is to create advocates, not philosophers. The
method emphasizes questions posed by the professor to a specific student
followed by a colloquy between the two from which the onlookers (the other
students) are to learn. These in-class dialogues may last only a few sentences
or many minutes depending upon the preparation level, rhetorical skill, and
courage of the individual law school student.

Inevitably, a new question on the same or another case will be posed to a
different student, and the dialogue will begin all over again. After multiple
unprepared, thoughtless, or illogical answers from the students in the class,
some law school professors' voices will harden and their temperatures will
visibly seem to be rising.

Some first-year law students dread being called upon for dialogue in
class. But there are important lessons occurring if you can watch, listen, and
learn. Why are some facts so important in one case, and not in another? Why
and how does the same question or issue get phrased differently in different
cases? Why does the same legal principle apply differently to different parties in different yet similar settings?

Learning to see why the professor is asking the questions she/he does, and how the sequence of questions is interconnected is part of the process of teaching you "how to think like a lawyer." The watching, listening, and learning here will prove invaluable when you are interviewing witnesses, meeting with clients, and/or responding to opposing counsel and the court in litigation.

During my very first Contracts class during my first year, first semester of law school, it took less than twenty minutes of dialogue for the professor to become convinced we did not read the cases with sufficient care and possessed no context within which to fit the common law principles of contracts. He put away the text and for the next two hours told a story with multiple variants (i.e., a law school hypothetical).

His story began with meeting a vagrant on the busy street just outside the law school entrance. The professor and the vagrant talked and entered into an oral agreement whereby the professor promised the man his overcoat in exchange for some specific performance. In two hours, by slightly shifting either his promises or the expected performance by the vagrant, the professor taught substantially all of contract law—offer, acceptance, consideration, quantum meruit, mutual mistake of fact, detrimental reliance, parole evidence, unequal bargaining relationship, and more.

Because I spent the fifteen years before entering law school teaching college students, I was mesmerized by this performance. I was so mesmerized that I failed to take a single note during the two hours and needed to spend the next hour and a half recreating what I had just witnessed.

That first class taught me a great deal. It made me see at the very start of law school why it becomes so important to see where questions were coming from and how they were interrelated. And it taught me that a student often does not quite see what a class is trying to do until after the class is over. From that point on, I tried to spend at least twenty to thirty minutes immediately after each class reviewing and elaborating my notes from the session.

9.5. STUDY GROUPS OR NOT

During the first two or three weeks of first year, there is often a mad scramble to form study groups. Study groups are usually composed of four, five, or even six members. While study groups are very popular, the danger I see is that study groups can have just as many "downsides" as "upsides." There is the "free-rider" problem as well as the differential effort and differential ability problem. If one of your group members is counting on getting through first year on the group's coattails, what are they bringing to the group's discussions?

There is also the dropout problem. Often study groups assign each member to become the group's "expert" in one class, for example Torts. If the first week in November your Torts expert drops out of law school or gets lured off to another study group, what do you do?

I think study groups can be very beneficial before final exams. Study groups in a particularly difficult course can also be useful if they meet three or so times during the semester to review the material taught and read thus far.

However, some study groups set up meetings multiple times each week all semester long. Sometimes these study group sessions turn into socializing or gripe sessions. Many hours can be spent not listening to the professors, not reading or rereading the cases, not working on your notes or building your outlines but instead listening to other students, who I suggest are likely to be just as stressed, confused, and unsure as you are.

Finally, many study groups assign each member to prepare a group "outline" for one course, for example, Property, and then all group members receive copies and use this outline to prepare for the final exam. Personally, I think this is a terrible idea and makes a first-year law student dependent upon four other students each semester for 80 percent of his/her GPA.

9.6. "THINKING LIKE A LAWYER"

The entire process of first-year law school, including the final examinations discussed in the following, is designed to train you to think like a lawyer. Coming out of college or university, many students learned to think critically and creatively. They tend to think big picture and to like big universal answers. They want results to be "just," or "fair," or "good."

But the law, and particularly disputes among litigants, is highly particularized. As Associate Supreme Court Justice Oliver Wendell Holmes Jr. noted, "[G]eneral propositions do not decide concrete cases." While college or university graduates in English, accounting, history, philosophy, or political science may want the law to establish logical and universal principles with invariable results, Holmes cautions, "The life of the law has not been logic, it has been experience."

Thinking like a lawyer requires accepting that every fact no mater how insignificant may impact a decision. It means that every minor change in language by a court may show a shift or drift toward an alternative result. It includes analyzing not just from one perspective—plaintiff's, defendant's, your own—but from many perspectives to understand what policy decisions are at issue and what experience with the law teaches about the issue.

Thinking like a lawyer in many ways is breaking down the big picture, service-oriented, value-laden education of your college and university career. Laws, law school will teach you, may not be perfect and may occasionally produce unjust results but are nevertheless both unavoidable and necessary. In your Contracts class when you reach the case of *Wood v. Boynton*, 1885, you will find a little old lady who takes a stone to an expert jeweler to determine its worth. The jeweler says, "I think it's a topaz." The little old lady agrees and they enter into a contract whereby the jeweler buys the stone for one dollar. It turns out that the stone was actually a diamond worth $700, a small fortune back in 1885. The lady tries to rescind the contract and get back her diamond, but the court rules that "mutual mistake of fact" without proof of "fraud" does not invalidate the contract and rules in favor of the jeweler.

Some young man or woman in the first-year Contracts class will raise his/her hand and state, "but that's not fair" and the majority of the class will laugh. They have learned to think like a lawyer. But the fact of the matter is that "it was not fair" to the little old lady, and there will later emerge in that same Contracts course escape theories and equitable remedies that can address the unequal knowledge and bargaining position, claims of expertise, and the like that could justify relief. There is an inevitable tension here. A law school cannot have everyone it graduates going around trying to do "right" as they see it. Rather they must be trained to know the law and to uphold the law and its principles.

9.7. OUTLINES

Since the casebook for each law school class will likely be four hundred to six hundred pages of densely packed material, it becomes impossible to study for the final examination simply from the textbooks. Most law schools recommend, and most law students prepare or purchase, "outlines" for the courses they take each semester. These outlines can be quite lengthy because they need to contain all the essential legal terms and principles (black letter law), the landmark cases, the variant positions, key factual distinctions, the legal rationales and alternative arguments, the policy issues, and any contemporary and classical trends in the area of the law.

Beginning the first week of law school (or even before), you will discover "canned briefs" and "prepackaged outlines" specifically for your casebook are on sale at the bookstore and online. You will find second- and third-year law students prepared to sell you copies of their outlines for the course where you are registered.

As indicated in the study group section earlier, I strongly believe that each law school student needs to prepare his/her own individual personal outline for each course. This requires a great deal of work and takes a great deal of time. But only actually briefing the case gets you to know its details, its reasoning, and its policy implications. Likewise, in preparing the outline you must organize, master, and reconstruct the course and its principles. The mere fact of writing or keyboarding the outline makes you remember the details and the contours of the problems addressed throughout the semester.

9.8. EXAMINATIONS

One of the most difficult adjustments to the first year of law school many students face is the lack of feedback, other than the daily cross-examination referred to as the Socratic method. While there is tons of homework, there is nothing to turn in or be graded. There are no quizzes and no midterms. Your course in legal research or legal writing likely will be the only area with written assignments. Everything hinges on the final examination.

Most law schools maintain archives of past examinations in torts, contracts, property, and so forth, and you will need to start looking at them after the midpoint in the semester. A few professors even give an in-class practice version of a final and then discuss how he/she would read it and grade it, without actually grading the students' answers.

The final examinations themselves are generally three hours long and require students to analyze a detailed, often meticulously/maliciously constructed fact pattern that will involve extended analysis and considering the problem from multiple angles. You can earn points for spotting the pivotal facts and the underlying issues, more points for methodically developing the analysis from more than one perspective, still more points for reaching a correct/defensible conclusion, and still other points for handling the policy reasoning underlying the analysis of the conflict.

The final examination could be one gigantic hypothetical with layer upon layer of issues involved, or a small number of hypotheticals each designed to cover a major section of the material treated in the course. Count on the examination, in whichever format, to essentially test everything you were to learn and more during the semester.

Today, most final exams are done on your laptop computer. Once you arrive at the lecture hall and log in for the exam, the law school's software programming effectively seizes control of your laptop and allows you to access the exam and only the exam. Notes, outlines, case summaries elsewhere in your computer files, plus the entire World Wide Web and e-mail, are unreachable until you complete and "submit" your final examination. Not having to decipher law students' handwriting made the lives of law school professors much more comfortable in recent years.

In addition, law school final examinations are graded anonymously. Students do not put their name anywhere on the exam. At some law schools, students use their social security number, but many law schools randomly assign each student a number for each set of final examinations. Unlike your undergraduate major where class participation and cogent discussion could often impress the teacher and perhaps even flow over into grading on an essay exam, here your performance in the classroom both for good and for ill has no influence on the sole grade for the course, the final examination. While this could be a good thing, especially if you had difficulty adjusting first year to your law school's version of Socratic method, it does ramp up the pressure to perform on the final examination.

The exams can be three or four hours long, an endurance contest much like the LSAT, and involve what the law professors call "issue spotting," in other words, were you able to peel away the irrelevant or less relevant materials to find and focus on the core issues? Do you see how the multiple issues in the problem relate to and impact one another? Can you explain the competing public policy rationales and why one principle or party prevails over another? All of this issue spotting, recognition of competing legal theories and policy analysis is evaluating (i.e., grading) how well you have begun "thinking like a lawyer."

9.9. LAW REVIEW

Nearly every law school publishes its own law review, generally four issues per year. Many larger, established law schools publish two or three law journals (i.e., the university law review, plus perhaps an environmental law journal, a journal of intellectual property, an administrative law journal, or the like). These law journals publish law student notes on recent leading cases as well as articles written by law school professors, legal practitioners, and others.

But you cannot just join a law journal. You must be invited or earn your way onto the staff. At some law schools, selection onto law review is determined solely by rank in class (i.e., cumulative GPA); at other law schools selection is based solely upon a write-on competition held late in the spring semester of first year. At most law schools, selection is based on a combination of cumulative GPA and a write-on competition graded by the current staff of the law review. It is common for the GPA to be rated 60 percent or even more. Invitations to serve on the law review can range from only twenty-five to forty students each year.

Each second-year student on law review is expected to write and publish a case note that will be extensively edited by one of the third year associate editors. The articles to be published, written by law professors and practitioners, are selected and edited by the third-year student editors. In the process, every member of the law review is expected to become an expert in the most current edition of *The Blue Book*, which is a uniform guide to legal citation used in law schools, courts, and law firms.

Serving during second year as a member of and during third year as an editor of the law review or one of your school's other law journals will make your legal resume stand out from the crowd. While law school may teach all of its students to "think like a lawyer," it does not teach them to "write like a lawyer." Participating on law review does, at least in part. Nearly all federal court clerkships and many state court clerkships go only to students who served on law review. Many of the mega, national, and international law firms exhibit a distinct preference for hiring students who served on law review.

9.10. SECOND-YEAR INTERVIEWS

Other things, like second-year interviews for summer associate positions and federal or state clerkships following graduation, also hinge heavily upon your first-year law school GPA. As discussed in the following chapter, almost all large and midsize law firms hire law school students completing their second year as summer associates of the firm. Often the larger the firm, the higher the summer associate salary will be. Prior to 2008, major firms paid in excess of $2,000 a week to summer associates. Following the Great Recession of 2008, both the number of summer associate positions and the salaries shrunk. And, as noted before, many of the largest national law firms exhibit a marked preference for students who worked on law review.

Hiring summer associates after second year of law school offers firms some benefits as well. Like professional sports franchises, the teams (here the law firms) purchase a two- to three-month "tryout" period during which they can evaluate each summer associate's dedication, intellectual ability, writing ability, and interpersonal and communication skills, as well as her/his "fit" with the firm's practice and culture. A truly successful summer associate "tryout" can lead a law firm to make an offer of employment prior to the beginning of third year, contingent obviously on continued solid performance during third year.

9.11. CLERKSHIPS

Not only the justices of the United States Supreme Court but every judge on the Federal Circuit Courts of Appeal and the District Courts in all fifty states hire law clerks each year, generally for one year, occasionally two years. Terms for law clerks begin the summer after graduation from law school and end the following summer. The same is true for almost all state supreme, intermediate, and appellate courts. There is stiff competition for these clerkships because of the training and experience they provide and the networking they nourish.

Clerks work in the judge's chambers and perform a number of essential functions: researching both new and arcane areas of the law, preparing bench and evidentiary memos for use by the judge, even serving as a sounding board for arguments and counter-arguments in difficult or troubling cases. Judges, therefore, depend upon their law clerk's ability to know or learn the nuances of the law and to analyze and write like a lawyer: clearly and persuasively. They also count on their law clerk's ability to maintain confidentiality. It is not surprising that almost all clerkships go to law school graduates who served on law review.

Working so closely together each day in the judge's chambers, clerks and their judges build up bonds of loyalty that tend to endure far beyond the time of the clerkship. Clerks often appear to become part of their judge's extended family. And judges, in turn, can be extremely important in assisting their clerks in finding their first "full-time" permanent legal position.

9.12. THE SUMMER AFTER FIRST YEAR

There are by and large no paying summer jobs for those completing first year. And you will not yet have been eligible for any of the law school's clinical programs that can build your legal resume. Nonetheless, you need concrete legal experience on your resume to compete for summer associate jobs after second year. Returning to your old summer job as a lifeguard, a waitress, or a file clerk will not enhance your resume.

One solution is to volunteer or intern without pay in a legal position for the summer after first year. This provides a chance for real-world legal experience, an opportunity to network, and the possibility of a new, perhaps important, letter of recommendation. Many district attorney's and public defender's offices provide such opportunities. Actively search them out. Family members who are lawyers or judges, as well as lawyers and judges who are friends of the family, can also provide such opportunities. Law firms in your town or sprinkled around your county seat, as well as local magistrates of family courts, can also provide you with opportunities to volunteer and gain experience.

Aim high. Remember you are trying to build your legal resume to obtain your first full-time legal employment. Most federal and state court judges, both appellate and trial level, rely upon their law clerks, generally men or women straight out of law school, to perform basic legal research and to prepare bench memos for the judge analyzing the facts of the individual case before the court and the relevant case law with regard to both evidentiary and legal issues. As noted previously, these clerkships are generally one-year appointments and turn over in the summer each year. The clerks completing their term need to study for and take the bar examination in whatever state they are seeking to practice. This requires at least two months of concentrated, uninterrupted effort. Many judges are, therefore, quite open to a summer volunteer position for students who have performed well during first year of law school.

Chapter Ten

Second Year

Returning for your second year of law school, the professors assume you are already "broken" into the workaholic routine of law school. Therefore, three hundred plus pages for the first week of class is normal. However well or poorly you performed during first year, this is now a make or break year for building your resume, networking, and obtaining that all-important summer associate offer.

10.1. THE CURRICULUM

Where the first year of law school contains almost all the required common law courses, second year focuses heavily on courses that will be tested on the bar examination following graduation and on code courses (i.e., how to read, interpret, and apply complex legislative and administrative codes). No longer are you reading common law cases on nineteenth-century contracts, tort claims, or property disputes. Now you are studying modern sales and corporations issues, from requirements contracts to director's liability. This year you must learn how to read not just court opinions but codes: the Uniform Commercial Code (UCC), the Tax Code, and the Bankruptcy Code. Second year also generally brings you to Evidence and the Federal Rules of Evidence with all their "hearsay" exceptions and permutations. It will also bring you to the Tax Code with Personal Tax (often called baby tax) and Corporate Tax (big tax) courses, along with Debtor-Creditor and the Bankruptcy Code. Almost every second-year law school student is required to take a course in Professional Responsibility or Ethics focusing upon the American Bar Association's Model Rules of Professional Responsibility, another kind of code. Finally, second year brings many students to legislation and the "canons" for interpreting statutes as well as administrative law with regulatory notice and comment "rulemaking" pursuant to the Administrative Procedure Act (APA).

From the second-year law school curriculum, we now turn to those out of class activities that can make your legal resume stand out and get noticed— law review, summer associateships, clerkships, moot court, and mock trial.

10.2. LAW REVIEW

Those law students completing the first year of law school who are invited onto law review often end up feeling they are carrying an extra course or two. They are expected to attend staff meetings, help in the production of four issues, write a complex case note, respond to comments and criticisms from third-year editors, and make revisions, often multiple times. In addition, they must learn (plow through, grapple with, and memorize) what is affectionately know as *The Bluebook*.

The Bluebook, now in its nineteenth edition, served since the 1920s and 1930s as the legal profession's style guide for all legal citation. It is used by law students, lawyers, scholars, and judges in every form of legal practice. Whether it's the U.S. Constitution, federal cases, state statutes, books and treatises, periodicals, agency regulations, or foreign or international materials that you need to cite, *The Bluebook* tells you how to cite it. As a member of the law review, one of your first tasks is to learn how to "cite check" potential articles, case notes, and research. No course in law school, with the possible exception of legal writing, attempts to teach this skill. Even if an elective course on *Bluebook* citation were offered by the law schools, almost no student would take it.

Despite its importance as soon as you begin legal practice, especially in litigation, carrying *The Bluebook* with you everywhere during second year while learning the intricacies of citation is not a "fun" exercise. But, if it's an Alaskan state court decision, a Supreme Court decision, or a Pakistani court decision, *The Bluebook* will tell you how to cite it. If it is a presidential executive order, legislation from the New Deal era, or a bill currently working its way through the senate, *The Bluebook* will tell you how to cite it. If it's an EPA or FCC regulation, a United Nations Convention, a ruling from the Inter-American Court of Human Rights, or a GAO Report, *The Bluebook* will tell you how to cite it. The last two editions even contain rules for citation to electronic case files, blogs and websites.

As you are learning all of this, you are also trying to write a publishable case note for the law review on a topic and area of the law you may have been assigned rather than selected. You are also trying to keep up in your classes, not fall behind with your outlines, prepare for summer associate interviews, and generally survive second year without letting your GPA, which played a major role in getting you onto law review in the first place, suffer.

Beyond "thinking like a lawyer" in the classroom, second-year students generally find that with their service on law review they are also learning to "write like a lawyer," even to "practice like a lawyer." Serving on law review sparkles on your legal resume and brings you additional legal career options. But for all the great benefits, it also brings a heightened level of work and stress that you must recognize and be willing to accept.

It is little wonder that the mega law firms, with the most pressure-packed schedules and the highest billable hour cultures, love associates who served on the law review. They were already trained to handle longer hours, extra stress, and the pressure to be letter-perfect for two years in law school.

10.3. INTERVIEWING FOR SUMMER ASSOCIATES

Large and midsize law firms begin their interview process for the selection of summer associates during the fall semester of second year. This interviewing process can begin as early as October. At this point, the only legal credentials you will have on your resume are (1) your first-year law school grades, (2) whether you made law review or another law school journal, and (3) any legal volunteer work obtained during the summer at the end of first year.

Hopefully, this reemphasizes how important your first-year grades and making law review can be to your career. Again, hopefully this underscores why, in my mind, law school needs to be approached as one year, one very intense year that needs 150 percent of your time and effort every day.

The summer associate interviewing process is lengthy, time consuming, and nerve-wracking for second-year law students. Obviously no law firm can interview at all two hundred ABA-approved law schools or interview every second-year student who desires to sign up for an interview. The law firms and the law schools negotiate to decide how many interviews a firm will grant at a particular school and how the students to be interviewed will be selected. Will the law school allow a major firm (perhaps the biggest firm in the area) to dictate the category of law students to whom it will grant interviews (e.g., law review only or only students with GPAs above 3.4)? Or will the law school demand that any interviews at its school can only be conducted on a "first come, first served" basis. Quite often there are some of each and often a mixture, where firms, based upon a review of resumes from interested second-year students, select fifteen or twenty students to interview while allowing the law school to determine how the remaining ten or fifteen students are chosen for interviews (e.g., lottery, first to sign up, and the like).

Interviewing proceeds in stages and occurs both on campus and at the firms. For the initial on-campus interviews, many firms send two lawyers, often a more senior partner along with a more junior associate. This initial interview may not be overly substantive, but poise, confidence, voice, eye contact, and appearance as well as academic performance and legal potential are all being evaluated. Each interview will last perhaps only twenty or thirty minutes, and the total number of interviews by a firm can be spread out over a number of weeks.

With a substantial number of law firms coming to the law school to set up interviews during October and November, this can be a hectic and stressful time. And the faculty teaching your second-year classes will not reduce their reading load or the speed of their course to accommodate you. After the initial interview, students promptly write their "thank you" notes and then wait for the hoped-for "callback" or second interview. Again, this will likely be at the law school and will be a more substantive legal interview. The second-year students being interviewed need to bone up on the particular firm, its clients, its major partners, its practice sections, and its culture prior to both interviews. Students who took notes after their initial interview will remember the questions posed to them and be better able to address them again if they resurface. Most importantly, based upon their research into the firm, students hopefully will be able to articulate why she/he appears to be a good fit for that particular firm's practice.

For the most fortunate of those students receiving callbacks, there is an invitation to visit the law firm and spend a few hours. Often this third and final step in the summer associate process will happen over the semester break when there is no class in session or early in the second semester of second year. You will arrive on time, impeccably dressed and groomed, with copies of your resume, and with a number of specific and carefully thought-out questions prepared in advance about the firm and its practice.

You will then "run the gauntlet." You will likely start in the office of one of the partners who interviewed you on campus. Following about fifteen minutes, perhaps less, that partner will escort you to the next partner's office, which could be the next office in the hall or two stories away. As you walk, you will be speaking to your host and trying to absorb all the activity around you. You may go through five to eight of these one-on-one interviews de-pending on the size of the firm; they will be with both partners (usually from multiple practice sections) and with associates. Most, perhaps all, of these lawyers will be members of the firm's "hiring committee." Every one of these lawyers will be preparing an evaluation sheet on your visit within a half hour of meeting with you.

Generally, at the close of the final interview you will be escorted back to the partner's office where you began. You will be asked how your visit went and whether you have any final questions. You will be escorted to the front door of the office and told that you should be hearing from the firm in a few weeks.

Now the waiting game begins all over again. Second-year students will be interviewing at multiple firms, if they have the opportunity. They are seeking to hone their interviewing skills and to keep their options open. Law firms, in turn, will be interviewing more candidates that they can offer summer associate positions to because they know students are interviewing at multiple firms and may accept other firms' offers.

This is the same dance and same waiting game you played with law school applications, and it is just as stressful two years later. Indeed, these summer associate offers may impact your early legal career more than the law school which admitted you earlier. Hopefully, you will receive the phone call asking if you are still interested in becoming a summer associate and, if so, a letter confirming the summer hire.

Summer associate positions for the summer after second year are critically important components of the long-term hiring process for both law firms and law school students. Large and midsize firms pay for the opportunity to test out a number of "lawyers in the making" who have completed two years of law school. The firms, in effect, "kick the tires" for about two months and then decide whether your work ethic, personality, intelligence, flexibility, ability to handle pressure, and overall character fit with the firm's culture and practice.

At the close of the summer, based on firsthand, day-to-day contact with you, these big and midsize firms are often in a position to make contingent offers of full-time employment following graduation to at least some of their summer associates. This reduces the pressure the firm's hiring committee faces at the end of the year. The process also allows some third-year law school students to return for a final year knowing they already have an offer of employment. It can be a win-win scenario.

But not all summer associate positions get filled on this cycle. Many summer associate positions cannot be determined in September, October, or November. This is especially true for federal, state, and local government summer associate positions which are tied to funding processes linked to the annual government budget cycles. Summer associate positions with EPA, DOJ, HUD, DOL, and others all work with these limitations. And state governments with balanced budget mandates often work on a fiscal year ending December 31 or June 1.

In addition, many nonprofits do not know nine months in advance whether they will be awarded grants or receive other funding that would allow them to hire summer associates. And many of these public or nonprofit

entities do not have the manpower or money for extensive on-campus interviewing. Rather, they often expect law school students to send in resumes,
transcripts, and cover letters expressing interest in working with the agency
or entity. This second round of interviewing can occupy a good bit of second
semester.

Whether you find a position with a law firm, a government agency, or a
nonprofit, for students finishing their second year of law school, this is often
their first opportunity to actually practice acting like a lawyer, accompanying
senior lawyers to meetings with clients, preparing legal memoranda for senior associates of the firm, researching the multiple sides of a complex issue,
learning to take a position and defend it with reason, logic, and civility—
even learning to benefit from their mistakes.

10.4. CLINICAL PROGRAMS

Today, almost all law schools have "clinical" programs for second- and
third-year law school students. Clinical programs move you out of the classroom and into actual legal situations with attorneys, clients, and problems to
be solved. Each clinical course usually strictly limits enrollment, fifteen to
twenty-five is not unusual, and is taught by a faculty member with expertise
in that particular area of legal practice.

These clinical programs can be great resume builders and offer outstanding opportunities for networking with practicing attorneys. Clinical programs
also build important practical skill sets that generally are not taught in the
classroom but which you need after law school. These skills can include
communicating with clients who may be disadvantaged or disabled, interviewing and fact-finding (it is important to learn that sometimes your clients
from the poorest to the wealthiest do not tell you the whole truth), public
speaking, negotiating with confidence, drafting initial pleadings and simple
legal documents, as well as learning some of the intricacies of the court
systems and the regulatory agencies at the local, state, or federal level.

The variety of clinical programs is immense. Depending on the size of
your law school, there could be a legal aid clinic where you could learn to
perform intake interviews, make referrals, and perhaps assist on matters in
local landlord-tenant court or family court. Other clinics might include assis-
tance with income tax preparation or advice on immigration law. There could
be a child advocacy clinic, a small business clinic, or even an environmental
law clinic. These clinical programs will be prominently advertised by your
law school.

Back in the mid-1980s, my law school offered a Federal Courts Clinical
program. I felt extremely fortunate to be one of fifteen students selected for
the program and to be assigned for a year to the chambers of a wonderful

jurist on the United States Court of Appeals for the Third Circuit. I received a firsthand opportunity to observe very smart people working very hard to be thorough, fair, and impartial—to do justice. With the judge's three full-time law clerks, I read the briefs of the opposing parties, performed research, and wrote bench memos for the judge on prisoner cases, medical malpractice and tort cases, as well as on the simpler contract disputes. I observed oral arguments and sat in on discussions in chambers regarding the opinions being issued by the various three judge panels. During those nine months, I learned more about the law and how to think, research, and write as a lawyer than at any other time in my life.

10.5. MOOT COURT AND MOCK TRIAL

Beyond law review, other legal journals, and various clinical programs, the second year of law school provides some outstanding additional avenues to build your legal resume and increase the odds of landing your first full-time legal position. Essentially every law school will have a moot court program, often integrated as a required part of the second year curriculum, as well as a mock trial program engaging in competitions with trial teams from other law schools.

Moot court offers a chance for law school students to develop and practice the skill of oral advocacy or what is often called appellate advocacy. Moot court does not require the preparation, examination, or cross-examination of witnesses, nor does it require the introduction of evidence or the interposing of objections. Moot court is modeled upon the oral advocacy that occurs before the Supreme Court of the United States or any of the Federal Circuit Courts of Appeals. Thus it teaches diligent preparation, poise, posture, self-confidence, thinking on one's feet, and parrying logical arguments in ways the classroom's Socratic method cannot match.

Based on either a pending appellate case or a hypothetical case modeled on one or more past appellate cases, students prepare for twenty to thirty minutes of oral argument during which they will be interrupted with questions from law professors, lawyers, or judges playing the role of Supreme Court Justices. You will prepare for your oral argument based on a "Record" from a trial court.

The lower trial court made a decision in favor of a plaintiff or a defendant. The jury ruled upon the factual decisions and evaluated the credibility of witnesses, while the judge ruled upon the legal issues, including the admissibility of evidence, objections to the evidence or testimony, the constitutionality of statutes, and the applicability of the law. The losing party then appealed the trial court decision.

Factual decisions are not open to review before the Supreme Court or the Federal Circuit Courts of Appeals, neither is the credibility of witnesses whom the appellate court did not observe or hear in person. But evidentiary rulings and legal decisions, including decisions on constitutionality, are all open to review so long as the issue was preserved for appeal.

Many law schools require that all second-year students participate in at least one round of moot court oral argument. Some law schools require students to argue both sides of the case, in separate proceedings, one as appellee and the other as appellant. Often the top students are then invited into an elimination competition through which a moot court winning advocate for that year is decided. The skills developed in this program are extremely valuable to legal practice. Moreover, winning or getting into the semifinal or final round of the moot court competition looks quite powerful on a law student's resume and helps in the interview process.

Mock trial is very different from the appellate advocacy of moot court and develops a different set of legal skills. Many high school, college, and university students participate in mock trial competitions. A standard case packet, either civil or criminal, will contain documents (personal, business, or public), witness statements (often in the form of depositions), physical evidence (medical reports, photographs, sketches of accident scenes, and the like), and copies of the applicable rules of evidence and prior case law possibly applicable in the jurisdiction.

Teams of students, some playing the roles of witnesses, others playing the roles of advocates/lawyers, prepare for and actually try the hypothetical case before a judge (usually a law professor) and a jury (usually other law students). Student attorneys make opening statements and closing arguments. They must also undertake direct examination of their witnesses and the introduction of evidence supporting their side of the case. In addition, they must cross-examine opposing witnesses and object to both the questions asked by opposing counsel and the admissibility of various documents, statements, or evidence.

All student witnesses and attorneys are evaluated on their poise, voice, posture, courtroom demeanor, eye contact, knowledge of the factual and legal details of the case, knowledge of the legal authorities and the rules of evidence, as well as their ability to handle pressure and to interpose and respond to objections. These are skills not taught by the Socratic method in the classroom. Once learned, however, these skills are quite useful in responding to law school professors during colloquy in the classroom.

Some law schools incorporate mock trial directly into a trial advocacy course. Others run a mock trial program as a voluntary student activity separate from any course in the curriculum. Often trial teams travel to competitions around the country, and just as with moot court, success in mock trial competitions, receiving best attorney or best witness awards, are great additions to any law student's resume. *U.S. News and World Report* ranks the top ten law schools for trial advocacy training each year, and while a few of the Tier 1 programs make the list, Northwestern and Georgetown for example, many of the top trial advocacy programs in *U.S. News* are at Tier 2 and lower schools. This is simply another reminder that in deciding which offer of acceptance you will choose you need to carefully consider your long-term goals.

10.6. ELECTIVE COURSES—WINNOWING DOWN OPTIONS

By the middle of second year, students will have experienced a wide range of law school courses—common law courses, code courses, constitutional courses, tax courses, business courses, regulatory courses, evidentiary courses, perhaps even labor courses, intellectual property courses, bankruptcy courses, or immigration courses. To your surprise, you may learn that you really love business courses and tax courses. Or, despite your longtime aspiration to become a prosecutor, you may discover you really don't like the combativeness of litigation or the often aggressive use of the Rules of Civil Procedure or Rules of Evidence. All of this is a natural part of the second-year experience.

You can accelerate this process of winnowing down your options by utilizing your electives to further refine your legal interests. You should consider using electives in second and third year to further explore and confirm your new interests and perhaps even to build at least a small degree of expertise in commercial law, criminal law, or litigation. Also be aware that most law students planning on practicing in the tax field continue past law school graduation to obtain a master of law (M.L.L.) in taxation.

During second year, many students feel it is important to take courses that are frequently tested on your particular state's bar examination but are not required at your law school, for example, domestic relations, local government law, trusts and estates, wills, and the like. While this may be a fine strategy for many students, it can be a bit misleading. The reality is that at the time of graduation from law school, you will not be prepared to take the bar examination in your state no matter what school you attended or what courses you took. Practically every single law school graduate needs an intensive prep course the summer after graduation prior to taking the bar exam.

10.7. COMPETITIVE, CONFIDENT, AND CORDIAL

Hopefully many good things happen to you during your second year in law school. Maybe it will be a solid, rising GPA in the top third of your class. Perhaps, you will build a good-looking legal resume showing a volunteer legal position from the summer after first year, and either law review, or a solid clinical program, or a moot court or mock trial success, or working as a research assistant for one of your law school professors. And, hopefully, you gained experience and found success in competing for interviews for summer associate positions with firms, government agencies, or nonprofits.

You should end the second year of law school able and willing to compete it is what you have been doing since day one of first year. And you should be confident in your newly acquired ability to analyze, to dissect, and to "think like a lawyer." And you should have developed the ability to disagree and discuss "civilly." The practice of law is a profession, not just a job or an education. You need to develop the ability to be cordial to all with whom you work, even those with whom you are competing to build resumes, get into clinical programs, or gain interviews.

10.8. SUMMER AFTER SECOND YEAR—SUMMER PARTNERS

Wherever you spend your summer after the second year of law school, those three months can be just as critical to your legal career as first year or second year of law school. This is the key opportunity to network and place on display the competitiveness, confidence, and cordially that a good lawyer will possess.

I often tell my undergraduate students, "You have three opportunities to make a first impression: your appearance, your speech, and your writing." For law school students, all three—appearance, speech, and writing—will be carefully observed and evaluated wherever you spend your summer after second year.

With appearance, whether you are a summer associate with a law firm, a government agency, a corporate legal department, or a nonprofit, you are in a "professional" setting and must both dress and act the part. Your appearance, including your mode of dress, posture, eye contact, handshake, style, and gait, both in the office and in multiple social settings are being graded. The baseball cap, hockey jersey, or well-worn sandals that you wore to class, if not every day, at least every week, are no longer appropriate.

In assembling a professional wardrobe for interviewing and summer associate positions, there are almost endless concerns. Is my suit too bland, or my tie too garish? Do I wear heels or flats? If heels, how high? Are colored shirts acceptable? Is my skirt too short or too long? What does "business casual" really mean? Is my handshake too firm or too quick? When I walk the hallway do I appear to be striding confidently or just rushing?

These concerns in the office are often complicated by a wide range of social requirements outside the office—lunch with partners and/or clients; softball games (partners vs. associates); group dinners at Italian, Vietnamese, or Indian restaurants; receptions with more than enough alcohol; weekend cookouts at a senior partner's home; invitations to go out for drinks after work. Even outside the office, these are still professional settings where you need to appear cordial, relaxed, and good company but behave like a member of the legal profession, not like a second-year law student escaping from the law library for the first time in two years.

Regarding your speech, the rule is communicate simply and effectively. No "ahs," "ums," "you knows"—no mumbling and no hesitation. In conversation be direct, be civil, maintain eye contact, answer what is asked, don't rush, and know when to stop. And, above all, never appear confrontational. Word choice says a lot about you, there is no need for big words when more simple and direct words do the job. Know how to ask questions and seek clarification when you need it. Pose the right issues to senior lawyers—it is like issue spotting in law school. And consider multiple sides of the issue being analyzed or discussed. Last, it is alright to say occasionally "I don't know" but "I will go find out"—lawyers young and old must do this every day.

Regarding your writing, first have read *The Lawyer's Guide to Writing Well* discussed in the section on summer reading after college or university graduation. Go back and reread at least chapters 3, 8, and 9 "Ten Steps to Writing," "Writing the Lead," and "Form, Structure, and Organization." Especially when you did not serve on one of your school's law journals, know basic *Bluebook* citation cold and check out any esoteric citation carefully. Legal writing is often so bad that short correct sentences, proper word choice, and clean, clear organization will impress.

Two final points need mentioning—"civility" and "commitment." Lawyers in private practice, government, and the corporate world work long hours, facing deadlines and pressure from clients internal and external. They need to be able to trust and enjoy the people with whom they work. In addition to evaluating your appearance, your speech, and your writing ability, everyone is also asking, "Would I enjoy working with this young woman or this young man five, often six, days a week for the next five years or more?"

If you display the necessary skills from law school, being "civil" and respectful in your speech and in all your dealings, not just with clients and hiring partners but with secretaries, paralegals, document clerks, associates, and other summer associates as well, will go a long way toward answering that question. In addition, making it clear you are committed enough to volunteer for additional work, are willing to stay late or come in early to help out, are ready to pitch in and go the extra mile will also be remembered when the end of summer evaluations are filled out by everyone with whom you worked.

Chapter Eleven

The Third Year

11.1. WASTE OF TIME? THE UNNECESSARY YEAR?

For a number of generations, law students have periodically claimed that law school should be only two years, not three. Students returning to law school after a summer clerkship whether with a firm, a judge, or an agency feel as if they received a "taste" of life like a lawyer and want to get on with it. This is especially true for those fortunate law students who return for third year with a contingent offer of employment in hand.

Some of those law school students adopt the "just get me through" approach, while others use the "hibernation" approach, feeling that the third year is a waste of time. This is a mistake. There are valuable uses to be made of the third year of law school, including developing your legal writing skills, building your legal resume, networking, polishing your job interviewing skills, and overall broadening of your legal vision.

Moreover, the reality is that the third year of law school seems destined to stay. In recent years, a few schools experimented with a two-year program, the most notable being Northwestern. But these programs generally do not drop the third year, instead they merely consolidate or compress the three years into two by starting first year in late May or early June and utilizing the entire summer after first year and in some cases part of the summer after second year. These two-year programs thus intensify the stress and demands of law school. And, since these programs still require the same number of credits, the students pay the same tuition costs and incur the same amount of debt.

11.2. ELECTIVES—HAS YOUR PASSION CHANGED?

Third year generally provides more elective choices than the first or second year. Use them wisely. Has your passion for one area of the law over another changed? Did your summer clerkship convince you that you really do love corporate law? If so, use some of your electives to develop more knowledge and competency in that area. Did your summer with a local judge convince you that you want to practice criminal defense? If so, compete to get into the clinical program with the Public Defender's Association, or with Community Legal Services, or even with the district attorney's office.

If you need to hone your legal writing skills, take a third-year research/ writing seminar on a topic of interest. This can be especially valuable for law school students who did not have an opportunity to serve on law review or whose summer clerkships focused on client interviewing and file management as opposed to legal research and brief or memorandum writing.

If you want a career in litigation, perhaps advanced courses in negotiations, alternative dispute resolution, or evidence are for you. Or perhaps you want to continue with the mock trial or moot court competitions discussed previously.

If you recognize that you are not at or near the top of your law school class and if not passing the bar examination the summer after third year keeps you awake at night, use your third year to take those courses which the law school does not require but which make up the bulk of your state's bar examination.

Finally, remember that most lawyers will practice in multiple areas during their career. No one can predict the "hot" areas of the law for 2020, 2040, or beyond. Nonetheless, intellectual property and the role of the Internet, especially on discovery and privacy issues, do not appear to be going away soon. International law will also likely continue to grow. Consider using your third year to take a range of electives that will broaden your legal horizons and expand your experience.

Instead of considering third year as "marking time" until graduation, use it to expand and flesh out your legal education and your resume as much as possible. The reality is that during the third year of law school and for the first two or three years of legal practice, you are still building your resume and your professional network.

11.3. STILL BUILDING RESUMES

The vast majority of law school students do not return for third year with an offer of employment in hand. Therefore, you must be using third year to build a distinctive resume setting you apart from the hundreds and thousands of other law school graduates who will also be looking for jobs. Since the Great Recession of 2008, third-year law students increasingly find obtaining their first full-time legal position more and more difficult.

It is nice to have a top quintile GPA and law review on your resume when you go for a job interview. But most of the class cannot do that. Nonetheless, everyone can make their resume distinctive. Success in mock trial or moot court, best paper in a research seminar, outstanding evaluations for two clinical programs, an offer from a state court judge to write a letter of recommendation based upon your volunteer work all help build a distinctive resume.

As I stated in chapter 7, I am never sure that faculty letters of recommendation for undergraduates really assist them in gaining admission to law school. Here, however, I do think letters of recommendation from law professors, one legal professional to another legal professional, do help you get interviews and, thereby, give you a better chance of being hired. That is why networking, through volunteering, law school clinicals, and law school faculty, is so important.

11.4. NETWORKING AND FACULTY SUPPORT

Many law school professors utilize student assistants who update calendars, answer phones, take messages, do basic research, pull cases, maintain files, cite check articles in progress, take roll, and otherwise assist the professor. Often these student assistants are third-year law students. These positions are great assets in building resumes and networking.

Law school professors, especially senior professors, taught hundreds upon hundreds of former students who are now in practice, often in the area. Many professors continue to have contacts at law firms where they previously practiced, and others keep in touch with judges for whom they clerked early in their careers. Law school faculty who trust your character, like your personality, and come to appreciate your developing ability to think and write "like a lawyer" serve as hubs leading out to spoke after spoke of personal connections within the legal community—at private law firms, public interest groups, bar associations, and court houses.

Never underestimate the importance of networking in the legal profession. Networking can be the key to obtaining new and keeping old clients. It can be the key to trust and good working relationships with co-counsel and opposing counsel alike.

Each time you volunteer or intern at a law firm, a judicial chambers, a district attorney's office, you need to be networking. Collect the business cards, learn about the office and its lawyers. Where did they go to law school? What is their practice like? What did you learn from being around them? Keep a record and keep in contact. For each clinical program you participate in during law school do the same thing. For your summer associate position do the same thing. And remember, the other summer associates, the ones you were competing with to impress the firm and gain an offer of employment, can in the next year become important contacts who can assist you with information about an opening at their firm or provide a positive assessment of your work leading to an interview. Law school friends who graduated a year or two ahead of you can do the same. Keep a record and keep in contact.

Also work with your law school's placement or career services office. Be certain your resume is perfect. Find legal and judicial alums from your law school. Read the law school's alumni newsletters.

11.5. EMPLOYMENT WITHIN A 150-MILE RADIUS

In that final scramble during third year to land a legal position following graduation, remember that most law school students find their first full-time legal position within 150 miles of their law school. Learn from your placement office which firms or companies historically hire graduates of your law school. Make a realistic assessment of your law school GPA, rank in class, and resume. Invite former graduates or young lawyers you have met while networking to lunch. Show them your resume and ask for honest reactions and advice. Learn from their responses.

Broadcasting eight hundred copies of your resume to every law firm, agency, court, corporation, and nonprofit in the area may produce broad coverage. But being able to write an individualized cover letter to specific professionals in your network with a polite request that your resume be passed on to the appropriate hiring committee or hiring partner may be a great deal more effective.

11.6. REMEMBER: YOUR DEBT MAY LIMIT YOUR JOB PROSPECTS

Never forget that your law school debt may restrict your job prospects. Not only do you need your first full-time paying legal position, but you need to earn a salary sufficient to begin paying down your student loans. Hopefully you addressed this reality in selecting your law school over three years ago and planned for the day your first loan payments come due. If you did not plan ahead, and now realize you are in a bind, you may want to focus your job search upon federal, state, local government, or nonprofit positions that while paying less will make your loans eligible for inclusion in the Federal Public Service Loan Forgiveness Program (PSLF).

11.7. SUMMER AFTER THIRD YEAR — YOU ARE NOT BAR EXAM READY

The goal for the summer after second year is to get real-world legal experience, make money, build your resume, and expand your network. For almost all law school graduates, the goal for the summer after third year is to prepare for the bar examination. Unfortunately, for many law school graduates this means incurring even more debt in the months immediately after law school. Today, there are loans designed expressly to permit law school graduates to pay for an intensive multi-week bar prep course, like Bar-Bri or PMBR (now Kaplan), as well as to study and prepare for the bar exam.

Most state bar associations have their bar examination the same week in mid to late July and it runs for two and in some cases three days. Pennsylvania, for example, holds its bar exam on the last Tuesday and Wednesday of July. One day of the exam will include the two-hundred-question multiple choice Multistate Bar Examination (MBE), administered in all states with the exception of Louisiana. The exam covers the standard first-year common law courses as well as the Uniform Commercial Code. The exam utilizes three hours in a morning session with one hundred questions and three hours in an afternoon session, after which most students feel that their mind has been pillaged.

The second, or second and third, day of the exam will be composed of essay questions utilizing hypotheticals not unlike law school final exams. There is a Multistate Essay Exam (MEE), but most states continue to create and administer their own essay exam based upon the peculiarities of their own state law. These questions can cover anything from agency, to torts, to secured transactions, to conflicts of laws, to criminal procedure, to family law, or constitutional law.

Since most law schools today consider themselves to be "national" law schools which seek to attract a first-year class from across the country, most law schools do not emphasize state law from the jurisdiction in which they are located. This underscores why almost every law school graduate needs a bar review course prior to taking the examination.

Finally, unlike the LSAT, which informs you of your score three weeks after the test, the bar examination taken in July forces you to wait until October to learn your score and whether you passed or failed. You can obtain bar exam passage rates for first-time candidates by law school and by state. It is not at all unusual for even the very best law school students to feel anxious and uncertain over whether or not they passed the bar exam.

11.8. YOU ARE ALSO NOT PRACTICE READY

Not only does law school not prepare you to take the bar examination, it also does not prepare you to practice law. No one teaches you how to recruit, treat, and coddle clients, much less how to track your billable hours or prepare bills. Keeping track of and reporting your time each day in six-minute intervals by client and matter number is a radically new experience for most new lawyers in private practice.

No one in law school warns you about the endless and apparently bottom-less swamps of discovery so many first-year lawyers are thrown into early in their careers. No law school course teaches you how to index, review, summarize, and manage thousands upon thousands of pages of documentation now primarily on CDs, much less how to work out discovery disputes with devious opponents and/or difficult judges. And no trial advocacy course prepares you for an outright misrepresentation by opposing counsel in open court, or for a client who withholds vital information from his/her own lawyer.

No legal research or legal writing course teaches you how to work cooperatively with secretaries, document clerks, court messengers, paralegals, other associates, partners, and the senior partners who compose the law firm management. And no legal research or legal writing course teaches you how much time to devote each week to staying current in whatever field you are now practicing in or that none of your effort and time counts as "billable time."

Moreover, most law school students essentially do no writing for their three years, except for final examinations. And in most courses, final exam points are earned for issue spotting, with a greater number of points for greater depth and breadth identifying the issues, the black letter law, the majority rule, the minority rule, and the legislative or judicial policy considerations leading to the conclusion. Errors in grammar, diction, spelling, sentence structure, and cohesiveness generally have no impact on the number of points gained. Many law school students actually leave law school with worse writing skills than when they entered. With the exception of one or two third-year writing seminars or the handful of students serving on the law review, law school students do not hone their writing skills while attending law school. Every law school student entering third year should buy and read a copy of *The Lawyer's Guide to Writing Well, Second Edition,* by Tom Goldstein and Jethro Lieberman.

The reading load for law school students, discussed in chapter 9, continues for lawyers in practice. But in practice much less of the reading is devoted to case law and much more is devoted to factual material—statutes, regulations, medical reports, corporate minutes, depositions, interview summaries, human resources manuals, trial transcripts, and endless document reviews.

Plus, the writing load for practicing lawyers is immense. Goldstein and Lieberman estimate in chapter 7 of *The Lawyer's Guide to Writing Well* that even a small law office may generate four hundred pages a week of memoranda, motions, briefs, opinion letters, settlement papers, contracts, wills, and the like. Words are the products of lawyers, and lawyers are in effect publishers sending their written works to judges, clients, and other lawyers.

The bottom line is that for the first few years of your legal career, you will be "learning on the job." Law firms, government agencies, and corporations all understand this and devote significant assets in training new lawyers to follow their institutional practices and culture.

Chapter Twelve

Lessons to Carry With You

What follows are seven simple lessons that I hope you can take with you following graduation from law school. None of them are profound; all of them helped me throughout my career. Perhaps one or more of them may help you.

12.1. LEARNING EVERY DAY

The first lesson to carry with you from law school is that one of the truly great things about the law is "lifelong learning." I still remember interviewing with a range of Philadelphia law firms in 1985 for my first full-time legal position. At every set of interviews, one or more of the firm's lawyers would emphasize what they were currently learning about that was new and interesting to them. During my own career, I found environmental litigation to be an amazingly diverse arena.

In one environmental case, you learned the chemistry and geology (hydrogeology) that explains how and why groundwater contaminated with a variety of chemicals moves through layers of soil, rock, and clay. In the next case, you learned how an oil refinery operated in Texas or how zinc manufacturing occurred in Illinois. One month you would be studying the cleanup of arsenic in an apple orchard in New York, and the following month you would be studying the cleanup of radioactive contamination at a nuclear site in Missouri. Over the years, I learned how commercial aircraft components were formed in Connecticut, how waste oil was recovered in Arkansas, and how munitions and gun turrets were created for the Navy in Minnesota.

I met with clients and witnesses who taught me about paint manufacturing, government contracting, and the proper handling of medical waste. Along the way, I learned about jet fuels, hair dyes, explosives, tear gas,

Agent Orange, chlorinated solvents, specialty chemicals, landfills, incinerators, wetlands, and circuit boards. For me, one of the greatest joys of practicing law is to be constantly challenged to learn new things and explore new areas.

12.2. CONTINUE TO PURSUE YOUR PASSION

The second lesson is to return to your passion. In the opening chapter, I encouraged undergraduates thinking about law school to continue to pursue their passion, whatever it was—dance, music, ancient history, biography, ballet, photography, sports, the Civil War, European architecture, psychology, anthropology, painting, hunting, whatever. During the three years of law school, far too many law students lose track of or totally give up the activities they were so passionate about when they began law school. The constant reading load, the pressure for achievement, the competition for success, the rush to build a legal resume, all combine to work against a typical law school student maintaining his/her passion for rock-climbing, modern dance, archeology, or contemporary fiction.

One of your first commitments to yourself after completing law school is to continue to pursue those passions that made you the unique person the law school wanted to admit in the first place. Those passions will actually make you a better lawyer because they will make you more human and, thereby, more interesting to clients, prospective clients, and other lawyers.

Once you get into your legal practice, you will quickly discover that the tiny facts and details of a case, project, or area of the law that you spend hours, days, and weeks developing, studying, and understanding are not very interesting at all to non-lawyers, including your partner, family, or friends. You became accustomed to using the words, concepts, and language presented to you in law school, you are "thinking like a lawyer," but to the rest of the world it all sounds like "shop talk," which does not really interest them. It will be your passions as a person, not your passion for the law or worse your passion for money, which will allow you to become successful landing and keeping clients.

At the firm where I spent twenty-two years, one partner loved live theater in London and Dublin, going at least twice each year for a week or more at a time, and he always had new plays and ideas to discuss. Another partner loved hunting, especially duck hunting, and would take current and prospective clients on wonderful trips to exotic hunting lodges around the country. A third lawyer loved classical music, especially Mahler, and had an amazing personal sound system assembled in his home. He would travel to Boston, New York, Philadelphia, or Washington to hear a Mahler concert. Others loved golf at The Merion Cricket Club or long bicycle trips or collected cellars of fine French wines. Every one of these men and women used their individual passions to get to know and impress clients and potential clients at lunches, dinners, and social occasions.

12.3. THINKING PROBLEMS THROUGH AND TRACKING THE DETAILS

The third lesson to carry with you is maintaining and refining your skill of "thinking like a lawyer." Your law school career trained you to think problems through from multiple angles and perspectives; you learned the importance of even the smallest details in a contract, a witness statement, a regulation, or an expert report. These are important legal skills to continue to hone and practice; they allow you to work in multiple areas of law and business over the course of your career. Indeed, these skills allow you to adapt to changing conditions and to take advantage of new emerging career possibilities.

This lesson, however, is a two-sided coin, especially for recently minted lawyers. Thinking like a lawyer means problem solving, competing, finding correct answers, developing winning strategies, creating win-win scenarios. The same skills that can make you a rising star at work can turn out to be counterproductive in your personal life. When you bring your legal skills home with you, you often discover your spouse or partner does not want you to "solve" anything but just to listen as he/she vents. Your children and friends may simply want time with you the person, not you the lawyer. And, as frustrating as it may seem to you, your family and friends, who are non-lawyers, will not be interested in the details you are immersed in at work. Once again, this emphasizes your need to continue to pursue those unique passions that make you special.

12.4. RESPECT, CIVILITY, AND PEOPLE

The fourth lesson is that to be successful and happy in your career as a lawyer, you almost have to be a "people person." While this is especially true in litigation, I believe it applies in corporate, labor, securities, personal injury, criminal, bankruptcy, immigration, and regulatory law as well.

Whether you are in a law firm, a corporate legal office, or a government agency, you will work on a daily basis with a range of colleagues and clients, other lawyers, paralegals, administrative assistants, witnesses, experts, and opponents. You will spend sixty or more hours every week interacting with these people, some of whom will be younger, some of whom will be older than you.

Thus, you will spend more hours each week involved in lawyerly interaction, than you will spend in personal interaction, with your partner, spouse, children, and family. The quality of your life over the course of each week depends a good deal on the quality of your daily life as a lawyer.

You will also spend a significant portion of your legal day working with or negotiating with other members of the legal and judicial community as well as opposing counsel and government lawyers or regulators in various federal, state, and local agencies.

One of the most common complaints about the practice of law for the past decade and more is referred to as a "loss of civility," the growth of ruthlessness, and outright hostility between parties and between lawyers. Each lawyer has the obligation to improve the civility of the profession.

During my legal career, I dealt with people at every level of society from janitors to general counsel, from chemical plant workers to corporate presidents, from truck drivers to self-employed accountants, from federal judges to librarians, from senior partners to billing assistants. If you accept that your job requires you to be a "people person," seek to learn from everyone you meet, and treat everyone of every station with civility and respect, including opposing counsel and regulatory authorities, your career will grow smoothly.

12.5. A PROFESSION, NOT MERELY A JOB

The fifth lesson to carry with you arises after graduation from law school and after you pass the bar exam and reminds you that the practice of law is more than a job, it is a profession. Upon passing the bar exam, you will be licensed by the state where you will practice, become a member of its Bar subject to its disciplinary rules and code of conduct, in almost all jurisdictions *The Model Rules of Professional Conduct*. Doctors also get licensed by the states within which they practice and have codes of conduct and formal disciplinary proceedings. Accountants, social workers, pilots, nurses, architects, veterinarians, and many others all have licensing provisions and professional associations.

But lawyers, unlike these others, have a formal swearing in ceremony, usually in court. At the ceremony, the new lawyers will be reminded that by joining the legal profession they are actually becoming "officers of the court." Indeed, the first paragraph to the preamble to the *Model Rules* states "a lawyer, as a member of the legal profession, is a representative of clients, an officer of the legal system and a public citizen having special responsibility for the quality of justice."

If you glance through the *Model Rules*, you will spot rules on Confidentiality of Information (Rule 1.6), on Fairness to Opposing Parties and Counsel (Rule 3.4), and on Truthfulness (Rule 4.1). In addition, the *Model Rules* seek voluntary service from every lawyer Pro Bono Publico (Rule 6.1). "Every lawyer has a professional responsibility to provide legal services to those unable to pay. A lawyer should aspire to render at least (50) fifty hours of pro bono public services per year."

12.6. DOING GOOD WHILE DOING WELL

For this lesson, I turn again to Justice Sandra Day O'Connor who reminds us that Alexis de Tocqueville concluded that lawyers were America's "natural aristocracy." In addition, Justice O'Connor reminds us that in 1787 thirty-three of the fifty-five participants at the Constitutional Convention were lawyers as further evidence not only that "lawyers have a responsibility to their community" but also that "they are uniquely capable of making a contribution."

Long before Tocqueville, Andrew Hamilton created a positive image of the professionalism and public spiritedness of "The Philadelphia Lawyer" by undertaking the defense of John Peter Zenger in his 1735 trial in New York. And John Adams, savagely attacked in the press for undertaking the defense of Captain Preston and his redcoats after the Boston Massacre in 1709, described his decision to serve as defense lawyer for the British as "one of the most gallant, generous, manly and disinterested actions of my whole life, and one of the best pieces of service I ever rendered my country."

Justice O'Connor ended her 1997 dedication address at the Washington University School of Law in Missouri with an admonition that law schools should make a commitment "to teach the importance of doing good while doing well." Whether law schools, in stiff competition with one another for the best 1L students and for the best legal placements for their graduates, will heed this admonition remains an open question. Nonetheless, it is clearly an important lesson for everyone considering law school or graduating from law school.

12.7. STRESS, SUCCESS, FAILURE, AND FAMILY

Many years ago, Joseph Story in describing the value of legal studies stated, "The law is a jealous mistress, and requires a long and constant courtship. It is not to be won by trifling favors, but by lavish homage." Story's famous quotation should provide newly minted lawyers just beginning their careers with both a lesson and a warning that is itself a final lesson.

The lesson is that expertise in the practice of law, whether you are a business lawyer, a personal injury lawyer, a tax lawyer, a prosecutor, or a divorce lawyer, only comes with experience and effort. Every lawyer will have successes and also failures; they are both part of practice. Hopefully, over time you will minimize your failures and maximize your successes. But you never eliminate failure and/or the potential for failure. Therefore, you need to keep learning and refining your practice each and every day, what Story refers to as "lavish homage."

But these demands generated by the practice of law create stress on lawyers both young and old. These professional stresses in turn put stresses on your personal life. Doctors will tell you how harmful stress from constantly meeting deadlines, seeking to please clients and partners alike, as well as competition that is no longer civil or professional can be to your health. Long hours, late nights, working weekends, responding to client demands even while on vacation can all be destructive to your personal relationships and your family life. The life of the law may be "reason" as Blackstone urges or it may be "experience" and not logic as Holmes argues. But the most important lesson to carry with you is that the law is not your life. Being a lawyer is both your job and your profession, but, if you follow my advice, you will have fed and strengthened your passions and remained the unique and interesting person who happened to go to law school and now is a good lawyer. You will never find it simple or easy to balance the demands of an intrusive profession with the demands of your life. But by striving to achieve this balance, hopefully you will be able to achieve Justice O'Connor's wonderful admonition "of doing good while doing well."

Appendix A—Four-Year Checklist for Those Interested in Law School

- Find an academic department you like and focus on getting the best grades possible. Law schools accept students from all departments and all majors in business and in arts and sciences. Your grade point average (GPA) is the second most important factor in law school admission.
- Get involved and active at the university: athletics, student organizations, campus ministry, volunteering. There are numerous legal and political groups at most colleges and universities (College Democrats, College Republicans, Moot Court Program, Mock Trial Association, Pre-Law Society, Legal Careers Night). Involved freshmen become officers and leaders in junior and senior year.
- Stay out of trouble. All law school applications contain questions which must be answered honestly about disciplinary violations during your college career. Failures in courses due to plagiarism, disciplinary action for a violation of the drug and alcohol policy, fights or destruction of property in the dormitory, having the police called for a disturbance at the fraternity house may all have to be reported.
- Locate where the pre-law program office is at your college or university and check out the available materials, introduce yourself to the university pre-law coordinator, be sure to have your name put on the pre-law program e-mail service list, and check out any materials posted online.

- Learn what lawyers do in their jobs. Lawyers work for law firms big and small, but they also work for government agencies, for corporations, for labor unions, for hospitals, and for service agencies. Talk to your relatives, neighbors, and family friends who are lawyers about what they do at their job and about what they like best and like least in their jobs.
- Ask yourself why you want to become a lawyer. Do you like to read? Do you like to analyze? Do you like to solve problems? Do you like to debate? Do you like to write? If your answers to any of these questions is "no," ask yourself again why you want to become a lawyer.

SOPHOMORE YEAR

- Continue to focus on getting the best grades possible. Never forget your grade point average (GPA) is the second most important factor in law school admission.
- Continue to be involved and active at the college or university: athletics, student organizations, campus ministry, volunteering. Look for and volunteer for leadership opportunities; involved students become officers and elected leaders in junior and senior year.
- Continue to stay out of trouble. All law school applications contain questions which must be answered honestly about disciplinary violations during your college career.
- Find ways to engage in community service (tutoring at neighborhood schools, Habitat for Humanity, the Appalachian Project, raising money for Haiti or the Gulf Coast). There are a myriad of opportunities for service at all colleges and universities.
- Start thinking about your credit (even if you don't want to). Law school is expensive ($18,000 to $45,000 per year for three years). Loans are available, but many students are leaving law school with well over $100,000 in debt (loans) which must be repaid beginning upon graduation. You will need a plan, and it's not too early to start thinking about it.
- Start thinking about letters of recommendation for law school. You do not need to approach faculty yet, but when you get back that paper with an A+ or that midterm that says "one of the best in the class," carefully save and preserve it so that senior year you can go back to the faculty member you have not had in class for a year or more and be able to remind them of just how well you did.
- Attend pre-law program meetings and programs. At a minimum, you will meet other students asking many of the same career questions you are asking of yourself.

- Continue to visit your pre-law program office and keep reading up on legal careers. Start reading up on the Law School Admission Test (LSAT) and on the first year of law school (1L).
- Make an appointment to sit down and talk with your college or university's pre-law advisor. Make sure you have a plan for getting into law school whether it is immediately upon graduation or after working for a year or two.
- Continue to talk with family, friends, and neighbors who are lawyers and continue to ask yourself why you want to go to law school.

JUNIOR YEAR (IN MANY WAYS THIS IS THE KEY YEAR)

- Decide when you will take the LSAT; everything else flows from this decision. Your choices are June after junior year or early October of senior year. Ideally you want to take the LSAT in June, get your score back by July, and have the remainder of the summer to think about what schools you want to apply to and to work on your personal statement. Your LSAT score is the most important factor in law school admission; some advisors would suggest your LSAT score is the dominant or overwhelming factor in admission.
- Commit to being fully prepared and taking the LSAT once and only once. If you are not fully prepared to take the test in June, admit it to yourself and get fully prepared for the October test.
- Decide how you will prepare for the LSAT: independent study, a study group, a commercial prep course, a personal tutor, or a combination of all of them. Past experience suggests that 250 to 300 hours of intensive study is necessary to perform well on this test. The LSAT is different from every other test you have ever taken, including the SAT; it does not test what you know or have learned. The LSAT's three components (critical/comparative reading, logical reasoning, and logic games) test your critical reading and logical reasoning skills.
- If you take a commercial prep course—Power Score, Princeton Review, Kaplan, Test Masters—recognize that you still must put in the 250 to 300 hours of preparation outside of class. No course can take the place of your preparation.
- Continue to focus on getting the best grades possible. Never forget your grade point average (GPA) is the second most important factor in law school admission. Take challenging courses both in your major and as electives; the law school admissions committee will be looking at your transcript course by course for only your first three years.

- Continue to be involved and active at your college or university: athletics, student organizations, campus ministry, volunteering. Seek leadership opportunities, run for an elected position, or volunteer to run a fundraising project.
- Continue to stay out of trouble. All law school applications contain questions which must be answered honestly about disciplinary violations during your college career.
- Continue and even expand your engagement in community service; there are a myriad of opportunities at every college and university.
- Continue to think about your credit; law school is expensive. You need a plan to pay for law school, and it's not too early to start thinking about it. Leaving law school with excessive debt may limit the type of legal practice you can afford to accept.
- Make a tentative list of faculty you might approach for letters of recommendation for law school. Continue to carefully save that paper with an A+ or that midterm that says "one of the best in the class," and preserve it so that senior year you can go back to the faculty member and remind him/her of just how well you did.
- Attend all pre-law program meetings and programs, especially those with law school admissions personnel. Read up on different law schools in the *ABA-LSAC Official Guide* to accredited law schools to decide which schools you might like to attend.
- Start making a list of what for you are the most important characteristics of a law school where you will fit in and excel: is it reputation, *U.S. News and World Report* rankings, faculty, class size, location/geography, student-faculty relationships, student collegiality vs. competitiveness, specific courses like labor law or environmental law, clinical programs, bar passage rates, employment rates for recent graduates.
- Regularly visit your pre-law program office and keep reading up on the Law School Admission Test (LSAT) and on the first year of law school (1L). Start taking at regular intervals full-scale former official LSATs and tracking you scores.
- Regularly sit down and talk with your pre-law advisor about how your GPA and projected LSAT scores correspond with the law schools you would like to attend. Continue to polish your plan for getting into law school whether it is immediately upon graduation or after working for a year or two.
- Study and learn how to use the Law School Admission Council (LSAC) website. Decide when you will open an account and register with LSAC.
- Visit career services at your college or university and learn how to create a professional-looking resume. Begin to construct your resume—no funky scripts or colored paper; this is to be "professional"—you are applying to a professional school.

- Continue to talk with family, friends, and neighbors who are lawyers and continue to ask yourself why you want to go to law school. Talk to former students of your college or university currently in law school about their experience during the first year of law school.
- Attempt to obtain a law-related "internship" or at a minimum visit a relative, neighbor, or friend who is a lawyer in their office and see if they would permit you to shadow them for a day or two.

SUMMER AFTER JUNIOR YEAR

- If you are truly prepared, take the LSAT in June during the summer after junior year. Your goal is to score as high as possible. If you score 160 you are in the eightieth percentile and if you score 164 you are in the ninetieth percentile. You must score at 155 or above; 155 is the sixty-fourth percentile. If your practice tests are scoring in the 130s or the 140s, you are not ready for the exam.
- If your practice LSATs show you are not yet ready for the official exam, recommit your efforts and make certain you are ready to take the LSAT in October after school starts senior year.
- Get your LSAT score back approximately three weeks after the exam (i.e., on or slightly before July 1).
- Once you have your official LSAT score, utilize the *Boston College Law School Locator* on the web to identify and make a list of all accredited law schools whose mean LSAT and mean GPA match your LSAT score and your GPA. Given the number of applications to most law schools, this comparison only tells you that you should be "competitive" or "in consideration" at such schools. Even if both your LSAT and GPA are in the upper half of scores accepted at a school, it is still no guarantee you will be accepted.
- Read up on all of the schools on your list in the *ABA-LSAC Official Guide* and start listing pros and cons from your perspective with each school.
- Whether you take the LSAT in June or October, utilize the summer to prepare a professional-looking (one-page) resume. Do not include high school awards or honors; do include summer employment, volunteer work for churches and others, co-ops and internships, and awards or honors while at the college or university.
- Whether you take the LSAT in June or October, utilize the summer to get a start on your personal statement. Many students find the personal statement to be the most difficult part of the application process after the LSAT. Do not provide a narrative of your resume. This is your one chance to "advocate" for your admission, and you are seeking to join an advocacy

profession. The law school faculty and admissions staff reading your personal statement want to find a reason why they should "want you" in their first-year class.

SENIOR YEAR (PLAN ON SEPTEMBER, OCTOBER, AND NOVEMBER BEING HECTIC)

- Before the start of senior year, you should be registered with LSAC's Credential Assembly Service (CAS) and have either taken the LSAT in June or be registered for the October LSAT. You need to register for the LSAT months in advance of the test to be able to be assigned to the test center of your choice.
- If you did not take the June LSAT, return to school fully prepared to do your best on the October LSAT.
- If you took the LSAT in June and have prepared your list of schools to consider applying to from the *Boston College Law School Locator*, meet with your pre-law advisor to discuss your options and begin to narrow your application options down to three categories: "safe" schools, "competitive" or realistic schools, and "reach" schools.
- If you are taking the LSAT in early October, you can still begin to identify and make a list of all accredited law schools whose mean LSAT and mean GPA match your GPA and your LSAT score as "predicted" by a sequence of full-scale practice tests on former officially administered LSATs. Typically, when they take the official LSAT, students perform three or more points below the average level they have been reaching on full-scale practice LSATs.
- Individual law school applications are all available online but generally cannot be accessed until on or about September 1. Access the applications for the schools you think you may be applying to and make a list for each school of the number of letters of recommendations required or accepted and of any and all essays which must be submitted in addition to your personal statement.
- Have career service personnel or trusted faculty and staff members review your resume and work to finalize your resume during September.
- During the first three or four weeks of the fall semester, make appointments with and contact those faculty members you plan to ask to write letters of recommendation for you. Ask, do not just assume. Provide the faculty member with the appropriate LSAC letter of recommendation cover form signed by you as well as a stamped envelope addressed to the LSAC Credential Assembly Service (CAS).

- Provide the faculty members writing letters of recommendation with a copy of your resume, a copy of your unofficial transcript, and the best of your exams or papers that you carefully saved from that professor's courses. You can also provide a copy of the form in *Appendix B*, one page of bullet points identifying what law schools are looking for in letters of recommendation. Provide at least a month lead time and follow up to make sure the letter is sent to LSAC in a reasonably timely fashion.
- Take the LSAT in early October if you did not take the June LSAT.
- If you are dissatisfied with your June score, and are retaking the LSAT in October, remember that most law schools average multiple LSAT scores. Thus, if you are unhappy with a 153 in June and retake the LSAT in October scoring 161, the schools to which you are applying are likely to be treating your LSAT score as a 157.
- Students taking the LSAT in October will not see their official score until on or about November 1, but will, nonetheless, have to find a way to accomplish all of the remaining tasks during October and November.
- During October, continue meeting with your pre-law advisor and read up on law schools to which you are thinking of applying. If the school is in your area, contact a student you know that is currently attending and ask to shadow that student for a day. By mid-October, you should narrow your list of schools to between five and eight with some being "safe," some "competitive," and some "reach" schools.
- During October and early November, you need to complete your personal statement. Spelling, grammar, punctuation, and diction must all be perfect. Have some people who know you well and whom you trust read the personal statement and provide honest feedback.
- Make final revisions and submit your personal statement to the LSAC Credential Assembly Service (CAS).
- During October and November, have all undergraduate official transcripts sent to the LSAC Credential Assembly Service (CAS). This includes transcripts from other universities, community colleges, or from summer courses taken at a different institution. Beginning in October, you will want to monitor your LSAC account online on a weekly basis.
- During October and November, complete any and all of the additional essays requested by the law schools where you have decided to apply. Answer the question being posed directly; those questions often seek information about why "you" are a good fit for "their" law school. A generic essay is easy to spot and unhelpful.
- Look at and make a careful list of all of the "disciplinary questions" on the applications you will be completing. Double-check with the office of your appropriate academic dean and with the office of the appropriate dean of student affairs to be certain your record is absolutely clean. Past indiscretions, especially in freshman or sophomore year, can be explained and

eliminated in a short addendum. Failure to disclose or worse direct falsehood will get uncovered, if not by the law schools which randomly check, then later by the Bar Admission Committee when you apply to sit for the state bar exam.

- Complete all of your applications online and continue to monitor your LSAC account to be certain that all essays, your personal statement, letters of recommendation, and your official transcripts are all in your file with LSAC.
- Submit all applications fully completed to all schools by Thanksgiving weekend. Most schools have rolling admissions and begin review of applications on or about December 1; a law school will not review an application that is not 100 percent complete. By meeting the Thanksgiving deadline, your application will be reviewed while the law school still has the maximum number of seats to fill in their first-year class.
- Don't relax yet; use November and early December to get caught up in all your fall semester classes. Never forget your grade point average (GPA) is the second most important factor in law school admission. In some instances, a law school will ask for an official transcript of your first semester senior year grades. If you do exceptionally well, you may want to send the additional transcript as a supplement to your application file.
- End of first semester senior year. Now you can relax until spring semester when you can worry about when you will hear from the schools to which you applied, make decisions about where you will attend, fill out FAFSA forms for financial aid, and worry about how you will pay for law school and how you will survive the first year.

Appendix B—Guidance on Letters of Recommendation

Letter of recommendation for_____. The student signing this form should provide you with his/her current resume, transcript, LSAT score, personal essay (if completed), and any other additional relevant personal information. Hopefully the student will also provide you with samples of his/her best work in your courses. You may find the following law school information useful in preparing your letter of recommendation.

- *Admission to law school has become extremely competitive.* This past year approximately 155,000 students took the LSAT. From 1997 to 2010, the number of applications increased by over 20,000 while the number of law school seats for first year students remained relatively stable.
- The *number of applicants* along with their *median GPA and LSAT scores* for the law school classes entering in August of 2011 *underscore the level of competition* students across the nation face. The following example is taken from the Philadelphia metropolitan area:

  - *Drexel*, 2,464 applications, 3.38 GPA, 159 LSAT for 147 first-year seats; *Penn State Dickinson*, 2,603 applications, 3.58 GPA, 158 LSAT for 155 first-year seats; *Univ. of Penn*, 5,811 applications, 3.80 GPA, 170 LSAT for 250 first-year seats; *Rutgers (Camden)*, 2,724 applications, 3.37 GPA, 159 LSAT for 189 first-year seats; *Temple*, 4,129 applications, 3.44 GPA, 162 LSAT for 258 first-year seats; *Villanova*, 3,110 applications, 3.49 GPA, 162 LSAT for 256 first-year seats; *Widener*, 2,000 applications, 3.15 GPA, 152 LSAT for 249 first-year seats.

- In the face of this competition, ***positive and detailed advocacy in letters of recommendation can often make the difference between acceptance and rejection***. The ABA confirms that most law schools are looking for a specific set of skills that will lead to success in law school. "These include **analytical and problem-solving skills**, **critical reading** abilities, **writing** skills, **oral communication** and listening abilities, general **research** skills, task **organization and management** skills, and the values of serving faithfully the interests of others while also promoting justice."

- ***Law school admissions officers*** assert that they are ***looking for specific and detailed facts*** demonstrating that a student possesses the skills to excel at their law school. For law school letters of recommendation, facts are the highest form of advocacy. *Identifying the specific paper, oral presentation, or exam* where the student excelled will set him/her apart from the thousands of other applicants. *Identifying the research project* where the student's insight, creativity, and analytical skills amazed and delighted you will make the letter memorable.

- Most admissions files are ***read by law school faculty*** who are looking for ***a reason why they should want this particular student in their first-year classes***. They care very little about majors or minors but care a great deal if a student takes and excels in the most demanding courses. They also appreciate any legitimate comparison you can make to recent graduates now succeeding in law school.

Appendix C—Successful Law School Application Strategy

A successful decision on where to apply to law school requires that *you be brutally honest when you evaluate your chances* of being offered admission to various law schools. Please carefully read the article *"Assessing Yourself Realistically"* on the LSAC website. Preparing a list of law schools to apply to is *not* an exercise about where you would "like" to go, or where you have always "dreamed" you would go, or "where your father went," or your uncle or your sister.

This assessment is also not about "who you know," not even about who you know teaching at or in the administration of a law school. And it is certainly not about alumni, donors, or politicians who attended a particular law school. This is not even about your belief that you must stay in Chicago, Houston, Philadelphia, Washington, or New York. *On the contrary, the process set out below utilizes hard data and requires you to make an honest evaluation of how competitive your specific credentials, primarily your GPA and LSAT, really are at specific law schools.* This process cannot guarantee you admission to the law school you have dreamed about for years, but if you are committed to becoming a lawyer, it is your surest approach to getting admitted to a law school.

1. Start with your *LSAT score* (the scaled score from 120–180, not the raw score) and your *GPA*.
2. If you transferred into your college or university after taking courses elsewhere, or if you have taken summer classes at another institution and transferred the credit in, or if you have retaken any course to improve your GPA, you will need to *recalculate your GPA*.

3. Some colleges and universities give credit for approved courses taken at other institutions but do not include those grades in the GPA calculation. And at many schools, if you receive a D in a first year course and retake the course earning an A, the school only counts the higher grade in your GPA. LSAC is not so generous and includes all grades in all courses from all undergraduate institutions when LSAC calculates your GPA for submission with your application to a law school. *To recalculate your GPA, as LSAC will, include all grades received in all courses, even repeated courses.* This recalculation will often lower a candidate's actual GPA. But this is the GPA that will be used by the law schools.

4. Next, go to the *Boston College Law School Locator* on Google. Utilizing the grid found there, *locate the box that matches your LSAT score and GPA*, recalculated if necessary. GPAs from greater than 3.60 to less than 2.60 are on the vertical axis. LSAT scores from less than 145 to greater than 165 are on the horizontal axis. If your GPA is 3.29 and your LSAT score is 157, that would lead you to box H on the grid. *Do not assume your credentials are competitive at every school identified in the grid at box H.* The twenty-six law schools listed in box H are listed based upon their seventy-fifth percentile and twenty-fifth percentile of both GPA and LSAT in last year's first-year class and are rank ordered from more competitive to less competitive.

   • *Example*: During a given year, Loyola Chicago, Ohio State, Seton Hall, and Michigan State are all in box H. Your hypothetical GPA and LSAT at 3.29 and 157 would fall between the twenty-fifth and seventy-fifth percentile for both GPA and LSAT at both *Seton Hall* (GPA 3.22–3.36; LSAT 157–161) and at *Michigan State* (GPA 3.21–3.64; LSAT 155–161) and thus would be **considered competitive** at these schools. Note, however, that your LSAT would be at the lower end of the twenty-fifth percentile at Seton Hall. At *Loyola* (GPA 3.35–3.75; LSAT 159–163) and *Ohio State* (GPA 3.34–3.81; LSAT 158–164) your hypothetical GPA and LSAT would both fall outside (i.e., below) the twenty-fifth percentile for both and thus would **not be considered competitive**, even though the schools are in box H.

5. *From the grid box* that matches your GPA and LSAT, *identify and prepare a list of those law schools at which your credentials will be considered competitive.* Keep in mind, however, that the ABA requires every approved law school to submit the twenty-fifth and seventy-fifth percentile numbers on its first-year class each year. And

each year, every school on the grid is seeking to improve its competitive position (i.e., seeking to elevate its twenty-fifth and seventy-fifth percentile).

6. Your next step is to *review the schools in the grid boxes to the right, to the left, and directly below* the box that matches your GPA and LSAT: for grid box H that would include boxes G, I, and L. Once again, *identify schools* at which your GPA and LSAT would be *considered competitive and add them to your list* of law schools for possible application. Do not worry about the length of your list or the geographic location of the law schools. You can whittle your list down later.

7. Continue this process to *add both "reach" schools* (those schools at which you may not be truly competitive but you have an outside chance and would love to attend) *and "safe" schools* (those schools where it looks as if your credentials will be found not just competitive but desirable). Identify each school on your list as reach (R), competitive (C), or safe (S).

8. *The Boston College Law School Locator is only an initial step.* The Locator does not tell you the entire range of GPAs or the entire range of LSATs that were accepted in the law school's first-year class. It also does not tell you how many people with approximately your exact mix of GPA and LSAT applied to the school last year or how many of those applicants were offered admission.

9. Next, go on Google and enter the *ABA LSAC Official Guide to ABA-Approved Law Schools* and here you will find the additional essential details. Identify each specific school on the list you prepared you wish to query from the alphabetical or geographical list of all ABA-approved law schools. On the *Official Guide* page for that school, you will find two buttons—one button for that law school's *ABA Law School Data* and the other button for a *Law School Description.* Each button will take you to two pages of information. *The Data pages will give you* information on the prior year's number of applications to the school, the number offered admission, and the number of first-year students who enrolled ("matriculated"). The *Data* pages will also give you information on ethnic diversity, faculty/student ratio, class size, tuition, and bar passage and employment rates. *But the real gold will be found at the very end of the Description pages.*

- *Example 1:* You must use both the Law School *Data* pages and the Law School *Descriptive* pages. From the *Data* pages at one of the schools where you felt you might be "competitive" you can learn that last year 4,434 candidates applied, 1,820 were offered admission, but only 214 enrolled. You can also learn that tuition plus expenses living at home are estimated at $29,947 per year. *The Applicant Profile Grid at the end of the Description pages is your key to making a good decision. This grid covers all LSAT scores and GPAs for all applicants to our example law school for the prior year.* LSAT scores from below 140 to 170–180 are on the vertical axis and GPAs from 3.75 plus to below 2.00 are on the horizontal axis. Just as with the *Boston College Law Locator* grid, you now need to find your exact spot on the example law school's grid. For each grid node, the Applicant Profile identifies the number of applicants with your GPA and LSAT who applied and the number who were offered admission. Using our prior hypothetical GPA of 3.27 and LSAT of 157, *the applicable grid node would be for GPAs from 3.25–3.49 and LSATs from 155–159. In this node, 307 students applied to our example law school last year and only 105 were offered admission.* You now see that only one out of three candidates in roughly your position were accepted; and in making a decision on whether or not to apply you will also need to recognize that while your LSAT would be in the middle of the node, your GPA would be at the very low end of the range, suggesting that your chances of admission may be less than one in three.

• *Example 2:* The far right of the grid for each school contains very useful information on all applicants regardless of GPA admitted with specific LSAT scores. Again utilizing the example law school Applicant Profile, it shows that *0 applicants with an LSAT below 145* were offered admission and *only 8 applicants out of approximately 800 with LSAT scores below 150* were offered admission. Only *54 applicants out of 733 with LSAT scores between 150 and 154* were offered admission (only 7 percent) and *only 366 applicants out of 1267 with LSAT scores of 155–159* were offered admission (still only 29 percent). When the applicant LSAT score gets into the *160–164* range, 1000 are offered admission out of 1334, or *75 percent.* And with LSATs in the *165–169* range, 415 are offered admission out of 455 or *91 percent.* **The lesson here should be clear.** Our example law school is seeking to build its first-year class primarily of students scoring at or above 160 on the LSAT. Obviously a few candidates with scores much like yours did get offered admission last year. But looking at all the data, can you truly believe you are "competitive"? **This is exactly the point to be brutally honest.**

10. *Between the Boston College Law School Locator Grid* and the individual *Applicant Profile Grid* available for most (but not all schools) in the *ABA LSAC Official Guide*, you can *build a list of schools* at which you can feel confident that *your precise GPA and LSAT were competitive last year.*

11. *Remember, applications are not free.* In recent years, application fees for individual law schools can be as low as thirty-five dollars (George Mason or Richmond), but most applications fees are fifty to sixty dollars, with higher-profile law schools, such as Boston College or Georgetown, having application fees of seventy-five to eighty dollars. These costs rise year by year. Registering for the LSAC Credential Assembly Service and each law school report you request increases your application costs. *Thus a student applying to only eight law schools could easily pay $750 or more in LSAC and law school application fees.* This is another reason to make certain that the bulk of your applications are being made to schools at which you actually will be viewed as competitive.

12. *Being competitive is still not a guarantee you will be offered admission.* Despite a student's best efforts, every year there will be cases where neither the candidate nor the pre-law advisor understand why he/she was rejected. *The overlapping, often identical-looking credentials of so many students make admissions decisions almost impossible to predict.* (If you sat on a law school admissions committee, how would you distinguish or choose between the candidate from a large university with a 154 LSAT, a GPA of 3.35, majoring in accounting and another candidate from a small liberal arts college with a 152 LSAT and a GPA of 3.53, majoring in English? What if there were fifty such candidates all with credentials between 152–154 and 3.35–3.53 and you could only offer admission to twelve of them?) This is why you are *advised to have at least two or three truly "safe" schools on your list* of schools to which you will be applying. It is very comforting to have been accepted at one of your safe schools in late January or early February while you and the rest of your classmates impatiently wait to hear from those two or three schools you really do want to attend.

To conclude, the process described here demands hard work, effort, and planning.

If you are committed to attending law school and beginning a legal career, these are the steps that can help get you there. If you have no idea what you want to do after graduation or simply think it would be neat to attend law school and refuse to consider any school outside your local area, perhaps you need to think harder about why you believe a legal career is right for you.

Appendix D — Additional Readings

Access Group. *Financing Your Legal Education: What's What, What Comes Next, and How to Do It* (New York: Access Group, 2010).

Arron, Deborah. *What Can You Do with a Law Degree? A Lawyer's Guide to Career Alternatives inside, outside and around the Law*, 3rd Ed. (Seattle: Niche Press Ltd., 1997).

Arron, Deborah. *Running From the Law: Why Good Lawyers Are Getting Out of the Legal Profession* (Seattle: Niche Press Ltd., 2004).

Ashar, Linda C. *101 Ways to Score Higher on Your LSAT: What You Need to Know about the Law School Admission Test Explained Simply* (Florida: Atlantic Publishing Co., 2008). Practical advice and solid common sense.

Breyer, Stephen. *Active Justice: Interpreting Our Democratic Constitution* (New York: Random House, 2005). Associate Justice Breyer is the latest in a long line of jurists following Holmes in seeking the democratic evolution of the law.

Deaver, Jeff. *The Complete Law School Companion: How to Excel at America's Most Demanding Post-Graduate Curriculum*, 2nd Ed. (New York: John Wiley & Sons Ltd., 1984).

Derbach, John C. *Writing Essay Exams to Succeed Not Just Survive*, 2nd Ed. (New York: Aspen Publishers, 2009). This short book by a member of the law school faculty at Widener has gotten strong praise from top law schools around the country.

Edwards, Linda. *Legal Writing: Process, Analysis and Organization* (New York: Aspen Publishers, 2006).

Estrich, Susan. *How to Get into Law School*, forword by Kathleen Sullivan, Dean Stanford Law School (New York: Riverhead Books, 2004). This book gets high praise from top-tier law schools.

Falcon, Esq., Atticus. *Planet Law School II: What You Need to Know (Before You Go)—But Did Not Know to Ask . . . And No One Else Will Tell You* (Honolulu: Fine Print Press, 2003).

Fischl, Richard Michael and Paul, Jeremy. *Getting to Maybe: How to Excel on Law School Exams* (Durham: Carolina Academic Press, 2009).

Goldstein, Tom and Liberman, Jethro. *The Lawyer's Guide to Writing Well* (Berkeley: California University Press, 2002). Your best guide to intelligible and concise legal writing.

Holmes, Jr., Oliver Wendell. *The Common Law* (New York: Dover Publications Inc., 1991). In these lectures, the associate justice describes how law evolves in response to changing conceptions of public policy.

Ivey, Anna. *The Ivey Guide to Law School Admissions: Straight Talk about Essays, Resumes, Interviews and More* (New York: Harcourt, 2005). Written by the former dean of admissions at the University of Chicago Law School.

Lammert-Reeves, Ruth. *Get into LAW SCHOOL: A Strategic Approach*, 2nd Ed. (New York: Kaplan Publishing, 2011). Includes twenty chapters addressing issues from "Evaluating Law Schools" to "Your Application Timeline," "Borrowing the Money," and "Students with Disabilities."

Levine, Ann K. *The Law School Admission Game: Play Like an Expert* (Santa Barbara: Abraham Publishing, 2009). A short book with good information on preparation of resumes and on writing personal statements.

McClurg, Andrew. *1L of a Ride: A Well-Traveled Professor's Roadmap to Success in the First Year of Law School* (St. Paul: Thompson/Reuters, 2009).

McKinney, Ruth Ann. *Reading Like a Lawyer: Time-Saving Strategies for Reading Law Like an Expert* (Durham: Carolina Academic Press, 2005).

Miller, Nelson P. *A Law Student's Guide* (Durham: Carolina Academic Press, 2010). This small book focuses upon the knowledge, skills, and ethics dimensions of a law school education.

Miller, Robert. *Law School Confidential: A Complete Guide to the Law School Experience* (New York: Saint Martin's Griffin, 2004). Written by students for students, it takes you from "Thinking about Law School" to "A Brief Review of the First Year Curriculum" to "Job Interviewing" during second and third year.

Montauck, J.D., Richard. *How to Get into the Top Law Schools*, 4th Ed. (New York: Prentice Hall Press, 2004). Includes interviews with law school admissions directors.

Munneke, Gary A. *Careers in Law* (New York: McGraw Hill, 2003).

Noyes, Shana C. & Noyes, Henry S. *Acing Your First Year of Law School: The Ten Steps to Success You Won't Learn in Class*, 2nd Ed. (New York: Hein & Co., 2008).

Nygren, Carolyn. *Starting Off Right in Law School* (Durham: Carolina Academic Press, 1997). Only one hundred pages that can teach you what thinking and analysis in law school will be like.

O'Connor, Sandra Day. *The Majesty of the Law: Reflections of a Supreme Court Justice* (New York: Random House, 2004). The first woman ever confirmed to the Supreme Court, Associate Justice O'Connor provides an overview of the evolution of the Supreme Court.

Owens, Eric. *Best 170 Law Schools*, 2007 Ed. (New York: Random House, 2007). Prepared for *The Princeton Review*, the first twelve chapters (forty-five pages) address issues like "Writing a Great Personal Statement," "Law School 101," and "Career Matters"; followed by lists of law schools ranked by category, such as, "Best Academic Experience," "Most Competitive Students," or "Best Quality of Life;" with two-page profiles on most of the ABA-approved law schools.

Parrish, Austen and Knolton, Christina. *Hard-Nosed Advice from a Cranky Law Professor: How to Succeed in Law School* (Durham: Carolina Academic Press, 2010). If you have been admitted to law school and you can only read one book on briefing, outlining, study groups, and final exams, this is the one to read.

Pound, Roscoe. *An Introduction to the Philosophy of Law* (New Haven: Yale University Press, 1922). These 1921 to 1922 lectures at Yale Law School display the tension in the common law regarding injury, property, and contract throughout the twentieth century.

Rehnquist, William H. *The Supreme Court: Revised and Updated* (New York: Vintage Books, 1989). A former Chief Justice tells how the Court does its work.

Scalia, Antonin. *A Matter of Interpretation: Federal Courts and the Law* (Princeton: Princeton University Press, 1997). A debate between Associate Justice Scalia and four professors on the proper role of the federal courts in a common law system.

Scalia, Antonin and Garner, Bryan. *Making your Case: The Art of Persuading Judges* (St. Paul: Thompson/West, 2008). If you don't know what a syllogism is or how to frame an argument, this book can teach you.

Schneider, J.D., Deborah and Belsky, Gary. *Should You Really Be a Lawyer? The Guide to Smart Career Choices before, during and after Law School* (Lawyer Avenue Press, 2010).

Sedberry, Steven R. *Law School Labyrinth: A Guide to Making the Most of Your Legal Education* (New York: Kaplan Publishing, 2011). Provides the perspective of a man who switched careers in midlife and excelled in law school

Shapo, Helene and Shapo, Marshall. *Law School without Fear: Strategies for Success*, 2nd Ed. (Foundation Press, 2009). This little two-hundred-page book includes discussions of "Briefing a Case," "Legal Reasoning," "Interpreting Language," "Studying and Reviewing," "Exams," and "It's a Mind Game: Psychological Tips for the Study of Law."

Staff of the Harvard Crimson, *55 Successful Harvard Law School Application Essays* (New York: Saint Martin's Griffin, 2007). A great way to get a sense of how a good personal statement should be developed. Just read five of these essays before you begin to think about your own personal statement.

Thomas, Clarence. *My Grandfather's Son: A Memoir* (New York: Harper-Collins, 2007). A memoir by Associate Justice Thomas on growing up in Georgia before the Civil Rights Movement.

Turow, Scott. *One L, The Turbulent True Story of a First Year at Harvard Law School* (New York: Penguin Books, 1977). This is a classic and a quick read about what the Ivys can be like.

*NOTE: The LSAC website contains an extensive bibliography of additional "Resources for the Pre-Law Candidate," which is divided into the following categories: Law School and Legal Education, Legal Profession, Biography, Jurisprudence and Legal Issues, and Financing Law School.

Afterword

I would be remiss not to thank the many generations of former students who considered law school as undergraduates during my two tours of duty at La Salle University and who are now successful practicing lawyers and law school students.

During my first tour as a professor and an advisor, I remember many hours of conversation about law school with Nick, Paul, Ralph, Chris, Brian, Phil, Michael, Richard, Larry, Greg, David, Mary, Bill, Barbara, Frank, Kelly Ann, Christine, Kate, Charles, Ellen, Terry, Noreen, Jane, Peter, Maureen, John, Lisa, Dawn, and Nancy. Each of them remains a valued friend to this day.

During my current tour as department chair and university pre-law coordinator, I have once again immensely enjoyed teaching and counseling an entire new generation of successful lawyers and law school students, among them Joanna, Maureen, Ricardo, Jaryd, Calvin, Holly, Chris, Kevin, Patrick, Mary Kate, Megan, Thomas, Julie, Tesla, Danielle, Mark, Shannon, Christine, John, Matthew, Michael, Mary Catherine, Haley, Brian, Steve, and T. J.

You should all know that each of you in some way added to the value of this *Handbook*. Indeed, the many questions you all asked and the long conversations we engaged in essentially created the framework and structure for this *Handbook*. My thanks and gratitude to each of you for your friendship, and I wish you continued success in the law.

About the Author

Michael R. Dillon, Ph.D. J.D., is a fifth-generation lawyer in his family and received his doctoral degree in political philosophy from the University of Notre Dame in 1970 and his law degree from the Temple University Beasley School of Law in 1985. He graduated law school magna cum laude and served on the Temple Law Review. He taught constitutional law to undergraduates from 1968 to 1985 and since 2007 has served as chair of the Political Science Department and as coordinator of the Pre-Law Program at La Salle University in Philadelphia. He currently teaches constitutional law, environmental law, jurisprudence, and political theory. From 1985 to 2007 he practiced law in the Litigation Section of the Philadelphia office of Morgan Lewis & Bockius LLP, one of the largest law firms in the United States. His practice emphasized environmental litigation, especially Superfund litigation, in federal courts across the country from Rhode Island, Pennsylvania, New Jersey, and Virginia to Florida, Texas, California, Tennessee, and Arkansas. For over forty years he counseled hundreds of students thinking about law school.